14 Secrets

to

BETTER
RELATIONSHIPS

Powerful Principles from the Bible

14 Secrets

to

BETTER RELATIONSHIPS

Powerful Principles from the Bible

Dave Earley

BARBOUR
PUBLISHING

Contents

Acknowledgments

We need each other. This book is the result of the lives and ministries of many people other than me. Many thanks to all of you.

- Cathy, you are my very best friend. Thank you for being such an encouragement and for praying over, editing, critiquing, and proofing every word.
- Daniel, Andrew, and Luke for your consistent encouragement.
- All the people I have "done life" together with in small groups over the past thirty years.
- All the people I have served alongside on ministry teams.
- The Barbour team for asking me to write this book.
- Paul Muckley, you are a joy to work with.
- Les Stobbe, for opening the door.
- Annie Tipton, for managing the in-house process, and Yolanda Chumney, for handling the typesetting.

Introduction

You need to have close relationships.

You want to enjoy close relationships.

You want to have the type of relationships that God will gladly bless.

You hope to love and be loved in relationships that hold through tough times.

Of course you do.

We all do.

And you can.

But you need to go about it God's way.

The God of Relationships

God is a relational God. As a Tri-unity, He has eternally existed in relationship with Himself. He created man and walked with him in the cool of the day in the Garden of Eden. He sent Jesus to restore the relationship between God and man, a relationship that was marred because of man's sin. God has witnessed every relationship in history and possesses infinite and perfect knowledge and wisdom.

The New Testament is a highly relational book. The letters to the churches (Romans, Corinthians, Galatians, etc.) were written to be read and applied in *community*. Gracing the pages of the New Testament are insights into how to truly "do life" together.

Christianity is a relational experience. A religion is a system of beliefs and external practices. But Christianity is more than a religion. It is a relationship with the living God that opens the way to better relationships with others. Tertullian, an early church leader, quoted the prevailing pagan view of Christians in the second century: "How they love one another and how they are ready to die for each other."

The prayer we frequently refer to as the Lord's Prayer—"our Father in heaven"—is a relational prayer. Note the plural, communal nature of the petitions: "give *us* today *our* daily bread," "forgive *us* *our* debts," "lead *us* not into temptation," "deliver *us* from the evil one" (Matthew 6:9–13).

The "one another" commands of the New Testament are relational guidelines. Throughout the New Testament, Jesus, Paul, James, Peter, and John give specific relational imperatives linked by the phrase "one another." Based on the umbrella command to "love one another" (John 13:34–35), the New Testament includes thirty-one additional relational imperatives, such as

"Be at peace with each other" (Mark 9:50)
"Wash one another's feet" (John 13:14)
"Be devoted to one another in love" (Romans 12:10)
"Honor one another above yourselves" (Romans 12:10)
"Live in harmony with one another" (Romans 12:16)
"Stop passing judgment on one another" (Romans 14:13)
"Accept one another. . .just as Christ accepted you" (Romans 15:7).[1]

Woven through these "one another" commands are *ancient, fundamental, nonnegotiable principles of successful relationships.* These "secrets" have served as the building blocks of successful friendships, families, and marriages for thousands of years.[2] There are many fine books that emphasize one or two of these secrets and help us to apply them wisely, but none of these building blocks will be as effective unless we start with a foundation of solid biblical principles.

14 Secrets to Better Relationships

Though all thirty-two of the "one another" commands are significant, many of them overlap. I selected thirteen of the most important (Accept, Love, Honor, Serve, Forgive, Be Honest, Encourage, Pray, Make Peace, Comfort, Invest, Carry, and Endure) and added a foundational assumption (Admit) to come up with fourteen practical, powerful people principles that cannot help but enhance and strengthen your relationships.

These fourteen "secrets," *if applied*, will help you become a better neighbor, friend, parent, grandparent, sibling, marriage partner, employee, or boss. The most introverted person can become a better "people person," and the natural extrovert can improve to become a master at relationships.

Suggestions for More Effective Relationships

1. *Read this book by yourself and prayerfully ask God to work these fourteen secrets into your life.*
I suggest you read it slowly, with a pen in hand, marking key ideas and making notes in the margins. Try to put into practice what you learn. Ask God to help you apply what you read.

2. *Read it with your small group or Sunday school class.*
Study this book one chapter at a time. Discuss how each member of the group strives to live out these truths in real life. Pray for each other. Practice what you learn as you "do life" together with those in your small group.

3. *Go back and reread this book annually.*
Most of the time, we *know* what to do—but we often need reminders. Relationships are too valuable to shortchange. Reread this book every year and keep applying what you learn.

Notes

1. Here are all thirty-two "one another" commands from the New Testament:

1. "Love one another" (John 13:34–35; 15:12, 17; Romans 13:8; 1 Peter 1:22; 4:8; 1 John 3:11, 23; 4:7, 11–12; 2 John 1:5).
2. "Be at peace with each other" (Mark 9:50).
3. "Wash one another's feet" (John 13:14).
4. "Be devoted to one another in brotherly love" (Romans 12:10).
5. "Honor one another above yourselves" (Romans 12:10).
6. "Live in harmony with one another" (Romans 12:16).
7. "Stop passing judgment on one another" (Romans 14:13).
8. "Accept one another. . .just as Christ accepted you" (Romans 15:7).
9. "Instruct one another" (Romans 15:14; Colossians 3:16).
10. "Greet one another with a holy kiss" (Romans 16:16; 1 Corinthians 16:20; 2 Corinthians 13:12; 1 Thessalonians 5:26; 1 Peter 5:14).
11. "When you come together to eat, wait for each other" (1 Corinthians 11:33 niv1984).
12. "Have equal concern for each other" (1 Corinthians 12:25).
13. "Carry each other's burdens" (Galatians 6:2).
14. "Be patient, bearing with one another in love" (Ephesians 4:2; Colossians 3:13).
15. "Be kind and compassionate to one another" (Ephesians 4:32).
16. "Forgive each other" (Ephesians 4:32; Colossians 3:13).
17. "Submit to one another out of reverence for Christ" (Ephesians 5:21).
18. "In humility value others above yourselves" (Philippians 2:3).

19. "Do not lie to each other" (Colossians 3:9).
20. "Admonish one another" (Colossians 3:16).
21. "Make your love increase and overflow for each other" (1 Thessalonians 3:12).
22. "Encourage one another" (1 Thessalonians 4:18; 5:11; Hebrews 3:13; 10:25).
23. "Build each other up" (1 Thessalonians 5:11).
24. "Spur one another on toward love and good deeds" (Hebrews 10:24).
25. "Do not slander one another" (James 4:11).
26. "Don't grumble against one another" (James 5:9).
27. "Confess your sins to each other" (James 5:16).
28. "Pray for each other" (James 5:16).
29. "Live in harmony with one another" (1 Peter 3:8 NIV1984).
30. "Offer hospitality to one another without grumbling" (1 Peter 4:9).
31. "Each one should use whatever gift he has received to serve others" (1 Peter 4:10).
32. "Clothe yourselves with humility toward one another" (1 Peter 5:5).

2. I refer to the biblical principles of relationships as "secrets" because these principles are tragically overlooked and underapplied.

1

Admit

Two are better than one.
Ecclesiastes 4:9

Life is mostly about relationships. When our relationships are going well, life is good. We feel full, strong, loved, and happy. But when our relationships unravel—or worse, don't exist—life is empty and lonely. We feel insignificant, insecure, weak, and sad.

We all have a relentless yearning to attach and connect, to love and be loved. This relationship hunger is the fiercest longing of the human soul. Our need for community with people (and God) is to the human spirit what food, air, and water are to the human body. That need never goes away. It marks us from the cradle to the grave.

"We are all just people who need each other," observed campus chaplain Reuben Welch. We need face-to-face interactions with others to be seen, known, understood, and served and to do the same for others. Jane Howard, in her book *Families*, says, "Call it a clan, call it a tribe, call it a network, call it a family. Whatever you call it, whoever you are, you need one."

Yet we live in a land of isolation.

The Land of Isolation

In an average year, more than forty million Americans will move. Put another way, every ten years, more than half the people you know will move away. The average American will move fourteen times in a lifetime, and the average worker will stay at a given job for just over three years. Americans move around so much that we find it difficult to sustain intense friendships. Many of us live rootless lives.

The wife of one executive whose corporation moved him every two-and-a-half years admitted, "To decrease the pain of saying good-bye to our neighbors, we no longer bother to say hello."[1] Add in the prevalence of divorce and the fracturing of the traditional family, and it's no wonder loneliness is now an epidemic.

One-quarter of all Americans will experience serious loneliness this month. Ninety percent of the male population in America lacks a true friend. Loneliness, according to Mother Teresa, is "the leprosy of modern society."

Isolation is both increasing and dangerous. Harvard researcher Robert Putnam reports that social connectedness is at its lowest point in history, and this loss of social capital results in lower educational performance, more teen pregnancies, greater depression, and higher crime rates.

Living lives of isolation has damaging results. Loneliness has been called "the most devastating illness of our day." Philip Zimbardo of Stanford University writes, "I know of no more potent killer than isolation. There is no more destructive influence on physical and mental health than the isolation of you from me and us from them."[2]

God's Solution to Isolation and Loneliness Is. . .People!

The evidence is overwhelming. We need each other! The persistent feeling of being unwanted, unneeded, unnoticed, and uncared for is something no one can live with. The Bible calls the medicine for this unhealthy condition *fellowship*.

What is fellowship? The Bible word for fellowship is *koinonia*. As a noun, it means "sharing together." Fellowship is learning to live life effectively with others. It is born and grows as we value relationships and admit that we need each other.

Secret #1
Value relationships and admit how desperately you need them.

Fellowship involves participating in relationships to the point where you get to know others and feel their hurts, share their joys, work together, and give a lift to one another. Chuck Swindoll writes that when real fellowship occurs, "Fences must come down. Masks need to come off. Welcome signs need to be hung outside the door. Keys to the locks in our lives must be duplicated and distributed… [and we must] share our joys and our sorrows."[3]

I used to think the only person I really needed was God. After all, He was perfect and He had everything I thought I needed. Yet after facing a series of severe physical battles, I discovered that I desperately needed other human beings as well. I needed their help, concern, understanding, and prayers. I needed community. I used to think community was a nice commodity, but I could do without it if necessary. I was mistaken. Community is an absolute necessity.

Relationships Are in Our DNA

From the first chapter of Genesis through the last chapter of Revelation, God speaks of our relational DNA. For example, Genesis 2:18 states, "It is not good for the man to be alone." From this text we clearly see that, even before the Fall, God said that isolation was not the ideal state. Humanity needed to be in community with humanity. Aloneness was not an optimum, healthy, or acceptable way to live.

In Genesis 1:26 God says, "Let us make mankind in our image." Note the use of the words *us* and *our*. They remind us that God has always existed in an eternal, triune community, named elsewhere in the scriptures as Father, Son, and Holy Spirit. All three Persons of the Trinity are separate, yet all are vitally linked as one. In other words, the "Great Three-in-One" is an eternal manifestation of intimate community and glorious *inter*dependence.

Genesis 1:27 states, "So God created mankind in his own image." Our being made in God's image points back to God's communal essence. As creatures made in the image of God, we also have a deep, unique, embedded relational identity. Yet instead of finding the fulfillment of our communal craving within ourselves, as God does within His triune essence, we find it in God *and* in one another. In other words, we not only have a "God-shaped void," we also have an "others-shaped void" etched into our hearts. We need other people. Life was not meant to be lived as only "Jesus and me." It was meant to be lived as "Jesus and '*we*.'"

Our relational hunger is an identifying mark of our humanity. We all have a relational gene and communal DNA. Bill Donahue and Russ Robinson write, "God chose to embed in us a distinct kind of relational DNA. God created us all with a 'community gene,' an inborn, intentional, inescapable part of what it means to be human."[4] Philosopher Dallas Willard says, "The natural condition of life for human beings is reciprocal rootedness in others."[5]

As humans, we are internally wired with a desire for connection.

Our craving for community is a reflection of our human-shaped void. No person can be complete without healthy relationships with other people. Community is what you and I were created for.

We Need Each Other

The New Testament contains several metaphors to help us understand the majestic and mysterious nature of the church. The church is referred to as a flock, an army, a family, a branch, and a bride; but the metaphor used most often is that of a body. Paul uses the word *body* thirty times in his letters to illustrate the functioning church. Nowhere does he use the term more than in his letters to the Corinthians. Why? Of all of the churches he planted, the one in Corinth was the most divided and the least healthy. One of the lessons he wanted to drive deep into their thinking was that they needed each other.

> *The eye cannot say to the hand, "I don't need you!"*
> *And the head cannot say to the feet, "I don't need you!"*
> 1 CORINTHIANS 12:21

Paul argues that just as different members of a human body could never make it on their own, neither can members of the spiritual body (the church) survive in isolation. We need each other. To think that we can get along just fine without others is both arrogant and unwise.

> *If one part suffers, every part suffers with it;*
> *if one part is honored, every part rejoices with it.*
> 1 CORINTHIANS 12:26

As John Donne famously said, "No man is an island, entire of itself." We are in this together. Not only is it impossible for me to flourish without you, you cannot flourish without me. You need me. I need you. We all need each other.

As a pastor, I saw the reality of the pain and problems of isolation over and over again. I have had people tell me, "I'll come to your church. I'll love God, but please don't ask me to get too involved with the other members. I'm not going to get close to anybody. You see, I got hurt and I need to heal." I understand what they are saying, but I definitely don't agree. Let me explain.

Your body is wonderfully designed to heal itself. Let's say that your right hand accidentally mishandles a knife and cuts a finger off your left hand. Which option would give that severed finger the best chance of healing?

Option A: **Remove the severed finger as far as possible from the rest of the body. Set the finger on a shelf until it is healed.**

Option B: **Reattach the severed finger to the hand.**

Obviously, Option A will fail. The severed finger will never heal on its own. Isolated from the rest of the body, it will wither and die.

Option B is the only wise option. The injured finger can only heal when it is reattached to the physical life that flows through the rest of your body. Amazingly, as the life flows from the rest of the body into the injured finger, it will heal and again be filled with life and vitality.

What is true of the finger physically is true of us emotionally, spiritually, and relationally. If we detach ourselves from a close connection to the body of Christ, our hurts will never heal, and we will dry up spiritually. God designed us for fellowship because we desperately need it and cannot flourish without it.

We Are Healthiest When Connecting with Others

A recent *Wall Street Journal* article states, "Increasingly, experts have been telling us how important social bonds are to well-being, affecting everything from how our brains process information to how our bodies respond to stress. People with strong connections to others may live longer. *The quality of our relationships is the single biggest predictor of our happiness.*"[6]

The need for others is dramatically played out when we consider physical health. One major study that tracked the lives of seven thousand people over nine years found that the most isolated people were *three times more likely to die* than those with strong relational connections. Even those with bad health practices but close relational connections lived *significantly longer* than people who were isolated.

Another study of 276 volunteers who were infected by a common cold virus found that people with strong emotional connections did four times better fighting off illness than those who were more isolated. Another study found that men who have many friends they can turn to for support are about half as likely to develop heart disease as men who have the least social support.

Dr. James Lynch, in his book *The Broken Heart,* observes that lonely people live significantly shorter lives than the general population. Harvard researcher Robert Putnam notes, "As a rough rule of thumb, if you belong to no groups and decide to join one, you cut your risk of dying over the next year *in half.*"[7]

Of course the emotional benefits of connection are immense. Dr. Larry Crabb stunned the world of Christian counseling a few years ago when he stated, "We have made a terrible mistake! . . . We have wrongly defined soul wounds as psychological disorders and delegated their treatment to trained specialists. Damaged psyches aren't the problem. The problem is disconnected souls. What we need is connection!"[8] Crabb further notes, "When two people *connect. . .*something is poured out of one and into the other that has the power to heal the soul of its deepest wounds and restore it to health."[9]

The First Christians Lived Shared Lives

The Christianity practiced by the first Christians was more than following a religion, ritual, creed, or doctrinal statement. It was a vibrant relationship with God *and* with each other. From the very first day of their Christian lives, the first believers dove deep into community with each other (see Acts 2:42). As Luke tells us in the book of Acts, "They *devoted themselves* to the apostles' teaching and *to fellowship*, to the breaking of bread and to prayer. . . . Every day they continued to *meet together* in the temple courts. They *broke bread in their homes and ate together* with glad and sincere hearts" (Acts 2:42, 46, emphasis added).

They put two types of meetings at the top of their priority list. They attended the large celebration times of teaching and worship in the temple courts, where thousands would gather at a time, and they met in smaller groups for fellowship in homes many times a week (see Acts 5:42).

These first Christians faced a world in which they were persecuted for their faith in the resurrected Messiah. They not only wanted to be together, they *needed* to be together. Though our culture is not quite as harsh as theirs, we still face storms in our lives. Chuck Colson states, "No Christian can grow strong and stand the pressures of this life unless he is surrounded by a small group of people who minister to him and build him up in the faith."[10]

Two Are Better Than One

Solomon was the wisest man who ever lived. He knew a bit about relationships. Think of it: he kept several hundred wives happy! Seriously, as king of Israel, he built a network of significant relationships with neighboring nations that brought his people unprecedented peace and prosperity. Writing under divine inspiration, Solomon pointed out several benefits of relationships.

1. Relationships Aid Accomplishment (Ecclesiastes 4:9)

Solomon writes, "Two are better than one, because they have a good return for their labor." In other words, two people working together are more productive than one person working alone. Have you ever noticed how some disciplines in life go easier when you aren't trying to do everything all by yourself? Maybe it's exercise or dieting or stopping smoking. Maybe we're talking about doing a ministry. It's often much easier if you have a partner.

Partnership aids accomplishment. A farmer had two oxen who were each capable of pulling eight hundred pounds, for a combined total of sixteen hundred pounds. But when he yoked them to each other and taught them to work together, they could pull two thousand pounds as a team.

2. *Relationships Enhance Encouragement* (Ecclesiastes 4:10)

Solomon writes, "If either of them falls down, one can help the other up. But pity anyone who falls and has no one to help them up." There will be times when we fall down. Isn't it nice when there are others to pick us up?

I love the Special Olympics. A few years ago at the Seattle Special Olympics, nine contestants, all physically or mentally disabled, assembled at the starting line for the one-hundred-yard dash. At the gun they all started out, not necessarily at world record pace, but certainly with the relish to run to the finish and win.

All, that is, but one boy who stumbled on the asphalt, tumbled over a few times, and started to cry. The other eight heard him cry. They slowed down.

They stopped.

Then they all turned around and went back. . .every one of them!

One little girl with Down syndrome bent down, kissed the fallen boy, and said, "That will make it better."

Then all nine linked arms and walked together to the finish line. Everyone in the stadium stood, and the cheering went on for ten minutes.[11]

3. Relationships Supply Necessary Heat (Ecclesiastes 4:11)

Solomon continues, "Also, if two lie down together, they will keep warm. But how can one keep warm alone?" Several years ago when our sons were younger, our family went on a vacation to Gatlinburg, Tennessee. One afternoon we were out hiking and got caught in a huge downpour. I have never been so wet in my life.

Afterward I put on my Super Dad cape and said, "Fear not, family—Super Dad will start a fire and dry our clothes. We can also cook hot dogs and marshmallows for dinner."

Unfortunately, our only wood had been soaked in the storm, making it nearly impossible to burn. Plus every five minutes one of my hungry children would say, "Daddy, when can we cook marshmallows? . . . Daddy, I'm hungry. . . . Daddy, why don't I see any flames in the fire?"

After two hours I was about to give up and take the clothes to the Laundromat and the kids to McDonald's. But I couldn't. After all, I was Super Dad!

I'll have you know that, yes, I went through an entire newspaper; yes, I used an entire pack of matches; yes, it took a total of two and a half hours; but we eventually had a fire. We cooked marshmallows! We ate hot dogs! We got our clothes dry!

How?

I remembered Ecclesiastes 4:11. After I got one stick to burn, I placed it near another and they both burned. Everything that burned got pushed next to everything else that was burning. That made the fire hotter and dried the rest of the wood so it could all catch on fire.

4. Relationships Provide Powerful Protection and Resilient Strength (Ecclesiastes 4:12)

Solomon concludes, "Though one may be overpowered, two can defend themselves. A cord of three strands is not quickly broken." Like it or not, we have a spiritual enemy who hates God and desires to hurt God's children. His easiest victims are those who are isolated from the others.

For example, a hungry wolf does not directly attack a flock of sheep. Instead it lurks on the edges, watching for an unsuspecting sheep that has wandered from the others. On its own, away from the flock, the stray sheep is defenseless against attack.

As a pastor I have observed the spiritual health of hundreds of people over the years. The ones who stay connected to the flock in healthy relationships make it through even the greatest seasons of adversity. The ones who break connection and wander on the edges are often crushed when sorrow comes. They are also the most likely to yield to temptation and fall into sin.

Solomon noted that a three-strand cord is nearly unbreakable. I've seen the same thing with sticks. A single stick can easily be snapped in two. Two sticks bound together are much more difficult to break, and three sticks joined together are impossible to snap. So it is with us. When we link our lives with others in close, healthy relationships, our ability to withstand temptation and survive adversity is hugely enhanced.

The Thing That Counts Most

Some time ago I was sharing lunch with Dr. Elmer Towns, vice president and cofounder of the largest Christian university in the world. He has authored nearly one hundred books, including a Christian bestseller and a Gold Medallion award winner. He has preached in the ten largest churches in the world.

That day Dr. Towns was about to mark his sixtieth birthday. When I asked him about it, he got a far-off look in his eyes and said, "As I get older I realize that the thing that counts most is not accomplishments, achievements, books, or speaking engagements—it is friendship."

Leadership expert John Maxwell said, "The basis of life is people and how they relate to each other."[12] Ted Engstrom, former president of World Vision said, "Without that time, effort, sweat, and tears [to develop truly great friendships], we could well miss out on life's greatest blessings."[13]

"I have never known anyone," writes pastor John Ortberg, "who failed at relationships—who was isolated, lonely, unconnected, had no deep friendships—yet had a meaningful and joy-filled life. Not a single person."[14] Richard Lamb writes in *The Pursuit of God in the Company of Friends*, "I came to see that God cared about my friendships. I grew to see that he cared about them more than I did."[15]

What Now?

You and I desperately need each other. Yet it doesn't take long to realize that healthy, strong, growing relationships don't just happen. They aren't quick and easy. They take wisdom and effort.

In this little book, I hope to show you God's wisdom regarding relationships. We will look at thirteen of the most important "one another" commands of the New Testament. It is up to you to add the time and effort needed to apply that wisdom.

Notes

1. Quoted in Charles R. Swindoll, *Dropping Your Guard* (Nashville: Thomas Nelson, 1982), 21.

2. Philip G. Zimbardo, "The Age of Indifference," *Psychology Today* (August 1980): 71–76.

3. Charles R. Swindoll, *Dropping Your Guard* (Nashville: Thomas Nelson, 1982), 22.

4. Bill Donahue and Russ Robinson, *Building a Church of Small Groups* (Grand Rapids: Zondervan, 2001), 24.

5. Quoted in John Ortberg, *Everybody's Normal Till You Get to Know Them* (Grand Rapids: Zondervan, 2003), 19.

6. Elizabeth Bernstein, "Making 2011 the Year of Great Relationships," *Wall Street Journal*, (December 27, 2010): emphasis added; http://online .wsj.com/article/SB10001424052970203731004576045721718177728 .html.

7. Robert D. Putnam, *Bowling Alone: The Collapse and Revival of American Community* (New York: Simon & Schuster, 2000), 331.

8. Larry Crabb, *Connecting* (Nashville: W, 1997), back cover.

9. Ibid., xi.

10. Quoted in M. Scott Boren and Don Tillman, *Cell Group Leader Training Participant's Guide* (Houston: Cell Group Resources, 2002), 10.

11. Adapted from SermonCentral.com, http://www.sermoncentral.com /illustrations/stories-about-Stumbling-Block.asp.

12. John C. Maxwell, *Be a People Person* (Colorado Springs: David C. Cook, 2007), 11.

13. Ted W. Engstrom with Robert C. Larson, *The Fine Art of Friendship* (Nashville: Thomas Nelson, 1985), 49.

14. Ortberg, *Everybody's Normal*, 30.

15. Richard Lamb, *The Pursuit of God in the Company of Friends* (Downers Grove, IL: InterVarsity Press, 2003), 17.

2

Accept

Accept one another. . .just as Christ accepted you.
ROMANS 15:7

Never Underestimate the Power of Acceptance

When my sons were in high school, an astounding thing happened every Wednesday night. A diverse mosaic of fifty or more teenagers piled into our house around 7 p.m. and stayed till about 9. They represented a broad cross section of the local suburban high school. There was the captain of the football team, an officer in the student council, the lead in the school play, and a cheerleader. There was a girl dressed all in black, with her hair dyed black and her fingernails and lips painted black. There was a drug dealer and a boy with incredibly long hair who obviously did not shower.

There were white kids, black kids, Latinos, Asians, Mormons, Muslims, and even a Wiccan. There were students from very wealthy families and ones from struggling single-parent homes. There were kids who were in the National Honor Society and kids who were on court-mandated probation. Most of the kids were from non-churched families.

Every Wednesday night during the school year, they gathered in our living room and kitchen to snack, sing, study the Bible, and pray. Cathy and I were amazed that they came consistently, behaved beautifully, listened, learned, shared, opened up—and came back again.

One night I stood at the door as they were leaving and asked each one why they kept coming. Beyond the expected lines—"to see my friends," "to meet girls," and "to learn about God"—was one I did not expect. Over and over they told me that they came because they "felt accepted." Then they'd add something like, "I can be myself," "I don't have to pretend here," and "I feel comfortable here."

As a father who has raised three sons through adolescence, who has pastored dozens of teens, and who now teaches college students, I have learned never to underestimate the power of acceptance. Helping others feel welcome, received, understood, and accepted is a powerful bond for better relationships. Whether it is parents helping their teenager feel accepted at home or employers making their employees feel valued or a wife accepting her husband without trying to change him, never underestimate the power of acceptance.

"All I Do Is Accept People"

Dr. Paul Tournier was a gifted Christian writer and therapist. Doctors from all over the world traveled to his home in Geneva, Switzerland, to learn from him. "It is a little embarrassing for students to come over and study my counseling techniques," he confided, "because all I do is accept people."[1]

Dorothy Bass directs the Valparaiso Project on the Education and Formation of People in Faith. She writes about a family that found a novel way to celebrate the principle of the Sabbath. On Sundays they had an agreement that there would be no criticism in their house. The result was that their children's friends ended up spending Sundays in their home.

Secret #2
Accept others as Jesus has accepted you.

Jesus Was the Master of Acceptance

1. Jesus associated with sinners

Jesus made it His practice to seek out hurting, broken, cast-off, disregarded nobodies and make them feel like somebodies. He let them know He accepted them even if He did not approve of their behavior. Though He was a popular rabbi (not to mention the holy Son of God), even notorious sinners felt welcomed by Him and comfortable in His presence. It changed many of their lives. But it drove the Pharisees crazy.

> *Passing along, Jesus saw a man at his work collecting taxes.*
> *His name was Matthew. Jesus said, "Come along with me."*
> *Matthew stood up and followed him.*
> MATTHEW 9:9 MSG

Think about what you just read—Jesus, the Jewish rabbi, invited Matthew, the hated tax collector, to join Him as one of His disciples. Matthew (also known as Levi) was looked down on and loathed because tax collectors not only worked for the hated Romans, they usually cheated their Jewish brothers out of money.

When Jesus called, Matthew followed. Following Jesus meant that Matthew would leave his well-paying job and comfortable lifestyle. But he went. Jesus was obviously the first rabbi to give Matthew something other than self-righteous judgment and rejection. Instead Jesus offered genuine acceptance of Matthew as a man. Never underestimate the power of acceptance.

Matthew wanted his friends to meet Jesus and experience the power of acceptance. As an outcast from his people, Matthew associated with people who also were outcasts, probably because they made him feel accepted. One thing I have learned as a parent, pastor, and professor: young people go where they find acceptance. Really good kids will hang out with kids who are doing really bad things *if* they find acceptance there. But, on the other hand, seemingly rotten kids can find transformation being around really good kids *if* the good kids will show them godly acceptance.

Back to the story. We note that Matthew must have made a good living and probably had a large house. So he invited Jesus and His disciples to join him and his friends for a dinner party. And Jesus went.

> *And as Jesus reclined at table in the house, behold,*
> *many tax collectors and [especially wicked] sinners*
> *came and sat (reclined) with Him and His disciples.*
> MATTHEW 9:10 AMP

Going to a party hosted by a tax collector was not something most rabbis would do, but it was not out of character for Jesus. Later we see Him inviting Himself to eat with Zacchaeus, another tax collector (Luke 19:1–6). The crowd judged Jesus for it (Luke 19:7). But Jesus' display of acceptance transformed Zacchaeus's life (Luke 19:8–9).

The Pharisees had no heart for such a radical departure from normal cultural practices; but rather than face Jesus head on, they went after His disciples with accusation and criticism.

When the Pharisees saw [Jesus] keeping this kind of company,
they had a fit, and lit into Jesus' followers. "What kind of example
is this from your Teacher, acting cozy with crooks and riffraff?"
MATTHEW 9:11 MSG

Acting cozy with crooks and riffraff? What an indictment! But they obviously were missing the point. Jesus didn't miss the opportunity to call them on it.

Jesus, overhearing, shot back, "Who needs a doctor:
the healthy or the sick? Go figure out what this Scripture
means: 'I'm after mercy, not religion.' I'm here to invite
outsiders, not coddle insiders."
MATTHEW 9:12–13 MSG

The Pharisees were legalists, people who believed salvation came by obeying rules. As a group, the Pharisees had probably started out with good motives. They wanted to be really holy guys. They thought the 613 commands of the Old Testament were not enough, so they added hundreds more of their own. They set the bar so high that no one could reach it. They believed that they alone had the inside track to heaven. And they looked down on everyone else.

They set themselves up as everyone else's judge. Their rule-keeping religion became their idol and slowly killed off their love for everyone else.

Anne Lamott writes, "You can safely assume you've created God in your own image when it turns out that God hates all the same people you do."[2]

Dorothy Day observed, "You only love God as much as you love the person you love the least."

The Pharisees loved external religion based on behavior. The Pharisees did not have welcoming hearts. As a result, they not only rejected "sinners," they rejected Jesus for associating with "sinners." Jesus had a welcoming heart. He accepted sinners because that was what ministry was all about.

2. Jesus lived with open arms

The incident with Matthew the tax collector was not the only time the Pharisees were upset with Jesus for associating with sinners. One Sabbath Jesus had been invited to dinner with a prominent Pharisee (Luke 14:1). In those days wealthy people's homes had a courtyard in the back, and the meal would have been served there. The invited guests would sit around the table with others from the community spread around the outside edges of the courtyard.

As Jesus healed a man with a chronic illness, the crowds got closer. When He told parables that revealed God's heart for the humble and hurting, they pressed in even closer to hear His teachings. This infuriated the Pharisees.

> *By this time a lot of men and women of doubtful reputation were hanging around Jesus, listening intently. The Pharisees and religion scholars were not pleased, not at all pleased. They growled, "He takes in sinners and eats meals with them, treating them like old friends."*
>
> LUKE 15:1–2 MSG

Notice their accusation, *"He takes in sinners and eats meals with them, treating them like old friends."* They hated that Jesus did not distinguish between people in the way they did. Jesus ate with Pharisees *and* He also dined with notorious and especially wicked sinners.

The verb "takes in" used in Luke 15 is from a root word meaning "hand." In today's language we would say Jesus greeted and treated people with an "outstretched hand and open arms." He welcomed, received, and accepted them. He gave them access to Himself. He invited them into companionship.

3. Jesus refused to cast the first stone

One day Jesus went to the temple to teach and a crowd gathered. Suddenly, bursting through the crowd, a mob of men came carrying a frightened woman. It was the Pharisees again, trying to trick and trap Jesus.

> *The religion scholars and Pharisees led in a woman who had been caught in an act of adultery. They stood her in plain sight of everyone and said,*

> *"Teacher, this woman was caught red-handed in the act of adultery.*
> *Moses, in the Law, gives orders to stone such persons. What do you say?"*
> *They were trying to trap him into saying something incriminating*
> *so they could bring charges against him.*
>
> JOHN 8:3–6 MSG

What could Jesus say? No Jewish rabbi would contradict Moses and the law. According to the law, an adulterer deserved death. But if Jesus said, "Stone her!" the crowds would never forgive Him. Wasn't He their champion because He preached mercy over religion?

At this point, the contrast becomes crystal clear. The Pharisees were about judgment, discriminating between people based on how the people did in keeping rules. They were about accusation and rejection. They were about following their agenda, even if it meant humiliating a broken woman and a young rabbi to do it.

But Jesus was about something more.

> *Jesus bent down and started to write on the ground with his finger.*
>
> JOHN 8:6

Jesus did not condemn the woman. And He didn't say anything to the Pharisees. He just wrote with His finger in the dirt.

No one knows for certain what He wrote, but I believe—since He is God and knows all things—He was writing the sins of the Pharisees.

"What sins?" you ask.

Maybe it was not big, outer, fleshly sins like drunkenness, adultery, robbery, or murder. But it could have been inner sins of the spirit, such as pride, self-righteousness, and judgmentalism. We could add deception to their list, because they obviously were deceived into thinking it is possible to love God and despise people.

And make no mistake, inner spiritual sins are serious, very serious. That is why C. S. Lewis said, "A cold, self-righteous prig who goes regularly to church may be far nearer to hell than a prostitute."[3]

Yet these blind Pharisees failed to see themselves accurately, were unwilling to see the poor broken woman, and refused to see Jesus for who He was. All they saw was their own position and that this backwoods rabbi was making them look bad—so they kept badgering Him to respond.

And He did.

> *When they kept on questioning him, he straightened up and said to them, "Let any one of you who is without sin be the first to throw a stone at her." Again he stooped down and wrote on the ground.*
>
> JOHN 8:7–8

His response stunned them.

"Go ahead and stone her. That's what the law says. But let the guy with no sin go first."

Ouch! They had not expected to have the tables turned on them. Jesus' words cut them to the quick.

> *At this, those who heard began to go away one at a time, the older ones first, until only Jesus was left, with the woman still standing there.*
>
> JOHN 8:9

One by one the self-righteous prigs dropped their heads, let go of their stones, and slowly walked away. They realized they were not qualified to pass judgment. They needed to put down their stones.

I wonder, do you have a few stones you need to drop?

John Ortberg wisely advises,

> *Put down the stone.*
> *This may mean that you need to take action:*
> *If you have spread gossip—go straight to the person you talked to, and apologize. Set things right.*
> *If your heart is hard toward someone—do an act of service for them. Don't tell anyone else. Ask God to change your heart.*
> *If you have behaved badly toward someone—go to them. Today. Ask forgiveness.*[4]

Life is much lighter if we don't carry stones.

Back to the story: Once the Pharisees were gone, all that was left was Jesus, the woman, and a pile of stones. Jesus could have used this as a teaching moment to show that He was the Holy One and ultimate judge of the universe. He could have picked up a few stones and hurled them at the woman. He alone had that right. But He didn't.

> *Jesus straightened up and asked her, "Woman, where are they?*
> *Has no one condemned you?" "No one, sir," she said.*
> *"Then neither do I condemn you," Jesus declared.*
> *"Go now and leave your life of sin."*
> JOHN 8:10–11

"Neither do I condemn you." To that woman, these words must have sounded like fresh raindrops after weeks of drought. The men were not able to condemn her. Jesus chose to withhold condemnation. He had no desire for her to die as a sinful woman. He wanted her to live as a godly one.

"Go now and leave your life of sin." Jesus extended to her the invitation to a new life—a life without condemnation, a life without lust and adultery, a life of transformation. Acceptance is a welcome reception for broken people to come, *and* an opportunity for them to be changed.

John Ortberg writes, "This is very important: *acceptance is not the same thing as tolerating any behavior.*"[5] We must learn to accept sinners without accepting sin. We must welcome sinners without condemnation, but also without condoning their sin.

4. Jesus was rejected so we could be accepted

Jesus' acceptance of sinners was without superiority, judgmentalism, or condemnation. It was extended freely and undeservedly. It was powerful because it called the recipients to a changed life. And it still does.

But it was also costly.

In eating dinner with the tax collector Zacchaeus, in welcoming Matthew as a disciple, in rescuing an immoral woman, Jesus made powerful enemies. They kept coming back until they found a way to kill Him.

Later Jesus was betrayed, abandoned, lied about, beaten, whipped, mocked, and pierced. He suffered the greatest agony as He took the sins of humankind upon Himself, as His Father judged Him and pronounced Him condemned. Then He endured the greatest act of rejection ever experienced as His Father turned His back on Him and crushed Him for our sins.

He was despised and rejected by mankind, a man of suffering, and familiar with pain. Like one from whom people hide their faces he was despised, and we held him in low esteem. Surely he took up our pain and bore our suffering, yet we considered him punished by God, stricken by him, and afflicted. But he was pierced for our transgressions, he was crushed for our iniquities; the punishment that brought us peace was on him, and by his wounds we are healed. We all, like sheep, have gone astray, each of us has turned to our own way; and the LORD has laid on him the iniquity of us all. . . .

> *By oppression and judgment he was taken away. . . .*
> *Yet it was the LORD's will to crush him and cause him to suffer.*
> ISAIAH 53:3–6, 8, 10

What Now?

> *There is now no condemnation for those who are in Christ Jesus.*
> ROMANS 8:1

> *Accept one another, then, just as Christ accepted you,*
> *in order to bring praise to God.*
> ROMANS 15:7

Jesus was condemned so you and I could be free from condemnation. Once we have experienced this astounding acceptance from God, we're enabled and obligated to pass it on to others. Since we, as broken sinners, have been invited and welcomed into the arms of our heavenly Father, we can invite and welcome others.

Notes

1. Paul Tournier, quoted in Ortberg, *Everybody's Normal*, 100.
2. Anne Lamott, *Bird by Bird* (New York: Anchor, 1995), 22.
3. C. S. Lewis, *Mere Christianity* (New York: HarperCollins, 2001), 103.
4. Ortberg, *Everybody's Normal*, 100.
5. Ibid., 102, emphasis in original.

3

Love

"A new command I give you: Love one another.
As I have loved you, so you must love one another."
JOHN 13:34

"How He Loved Him!"

These four words summarize Jesus' lifestyle and give us the secret of His influence. Jesus was notorious for His love. The words "how He loved him" were uttered by Jesus' enemies, regarding His obvious concern for His friends—especially Lazarus, who had died.

> *Now Jesus loved Martha and her sister and Lazarus. . . .*
> *When Jesus saw [Martha] weeping, and the Jews who had*
> *come along with her also weeping, he was deeply moved in spirit and*
> *troubled. . . . Jesus wept. Then the Jews said, "See **how he loved him!**"*
> JOHN 11:5, 33–36 (EMPHASIS ADDED)

In order to escape the crowds and persecution of Jerusalem, Jesus often retired to the home of Lazarus, Mary, and Martha, located in Bethany on the outskirts of Jerusalem. It is interesting that this observation—that Jesus loved His friends—is lodged in the story of Jesus' raising Lazarus from the dead.

That Jesus loved deeply was evident. After arriving and finding Lazarus dead and Mary and Martha in mourning, He was "deeply moved." He was "troubled." He "wept." Those observing the scene had only one response—"See how he loved him!" What a statement. If we hope to be healthy people with good relationships, we need to be like Jesus. We must be people of evident love.

Secret #3
Love.

Jesus Loved People

Jesus is our model of healthy humanity, and He is the master of relationships. A quick read through the Gospels makes it clear— Jesus loved people.

1. Jesus loved the hurting and hopeless
When He saw the crowds, it broke His heart.

> *When he saw the crowds, he had compassion on them, because*
> *they were harassed and helpless, like sheep without a shepherd.*
>
> MATTHEW 9:36

2. Jesus loved spiritual seekers
Mark records Jesus' interaction with a wealthy young man. He notes, "Jesus looked at him and *loved* him" (Mark 10:21, emphasis added).

3. Jesus loved His disciples
For example, the apostle John was one of the most influential men in church history. Yet he chose always to refer to himself in one way—"the disciple whom Jesus loved" (John 13:23; 19:26; 20:2; 21:7, 20).

Jesus had an expectation that His disciples would love others based on His love for them. Note how many times the word *love* is used in just one section of Jesus' teaching on the vine and the branches:

> *As the Father has **loved** Me, so have I **loved** you. Abide in my **love**.*
> *If you keep my commandments, you will abide in my **love**, just as I have*
> *kept my Father's commandments and abide in his **love**. . . . This is my*

*commandment, that you **love** one another as I have **loved** you. Greater **love**
has no one than this, that someone lay down his life for his friends. . . .
These things I command you, so that you will **love** one another.*
JOHN 15:9–10, 12–13, 17 ESV (EMPHASIS ADDED)

It Is All about Love

As His ministry moved to the climax of Calvary, Jesus' dealings
with religious leaders intensified. They began to question Him,
hoping to trap Him in words and expose Him as a fake. Of course,
they failed.

On one such occasion, the question had to do with the
greatest commandment. The Old Testament includes more than
six hundred, to which the Pharisees had added hundreds of others.
How could Jesus pick just one? Even if He did, the Pharisees
reasoned, it would devalue the others. They thought this approach
would work.

Yet with piercing insight, Jesus answered their question and
summarized the entire law in two commands, both focused on
love.

*When the Pharisees heard that [Jesus] had silenced the Sadducees,
they gathered together. And one of them, a lawyer, asked him a question
to test him. "Teacher, which is the great commandment in the Law?"
And he said to him, "You shall **love the Lord your God** with all your heart*

49

> *and with all your soul and with all your mind. This is the*
> *great and first commandment. And a second is like it:*
> *You shall **love your neighbor as yourself**. On these*
> *two commandments depend all the Law and the Prophets."*
> Matthew 22:34–40 esv (emphasis added)

Jesus cut through the external trappings of religion and revealed the law of God in its purest sense: life is all about love.

"Love One Another"

Jesus *commanded* His followers to love one another:

> *"A new command I give you: **Love one another**. As I have*
> *loved you, so you must **love one another**. By this everyone*
> *will know that you are my disciples, if you **love one another**."*
> John 13:34–35 (emphasis added)

Note that He said that we are to love one another *as He has loved us.* Jesus loves us with an absolute, amazing, astounding, unearned love. His love is very precious—and was extremely costly. He loved us while we were yet sinners (Romans 5:8).

You and I can consistently have such love only by allowing Him to love others through us. It is a fruit of His Spirit that springs forth as we yield our lives to Him (Galatians 5:22–23).

The command to "love one another" must become our lifestyle. It is so significant that it is repeated ten times in the New Testament. (John 13:34–35; 15:12, 17; 1 John 3:11, 23; 4:7, 11–12; 2 John 1:5). Peter and Paul also remind us of this important command (Romans 13:8; 1 Peter 1:22; 4:8).

Every Christian is obligated to love others because that's what we've been commanded by Jesus. Every person who wants to enjoy better relationships will love others, because that is the example set by Jesus. So we might reasonably ask: What does it look like to love people as Jesus has loved us? Consider five descriptions of love.

Love Is. . .

1. Love is an expression

Love, like faith, does not exist until it is expressed. Jesus expressed His love for His disciples by taking action and washing their feet.

> *Now before the Feast of the Passover, when Jesus knew that His hour had come that He should depart from this world to the Father, having **loved** His own who were in the world, He **loved** them to the end. . . . Jesus. . . **rose** from supper and **laid aside** His garments, **took** a towel and **girded** Himself. After that, He **poured** water into a basin and **began to wash** the disciples' feet, and **to wipe** them with the towel with which He was girded.*
> JOHN 13:1, 3–5 NKJV (EMPHASIS ADDED)

The love of Jesus was actively expressed. He actively served His disciples. Love is more than nice thoughts or words. It is active expression.

2. Love is a decision

I admit that I used to struggle with loving others because I did not always *feel* like loving them. Then I noticed the command Jesus gave us to love our *enemies*. I realized that no one feels love for an enemy. Yet God can command us to love them because love is more than a feeling. It is a choice.

> *"But I say to you who hear:* **Love your enemies***, do good to those who hate you, bless those who curse you, and pray for those who spitefully use you. To him who strikes you on the one cheek, offer the other also. And from him who takes away your cloak, do not withhold your tunic either. Give to everyone who asks of you. And from him who takes away your goods do not ask them back."*
> LUKE 6:27–30 NKJV (EMPHASIS ADDED)

Repeatedly God commands us to love each other. You can't command an emotion. Love is not merely an emotion. It is a choice.

3. Love is an ability

Recently I noticed a little prayer Paul offered in behalf of the Thessalonians.

> *May the Lord make your love **increase and overflow** for*
> *each other and for everyone else, just as ours does for you.*
> 1 THESSALONIANS 3:12 (EMPHASIS ADDED)

He prayed for their love to "increase and overflow." This implies that love is something that can be developed and cultivated.

As an example, think of learning to play the piano. When you first start to play, you're not very good. You are restricted to your beginner's music. It does not come easily. Yet as you practice over and over, day after day, you improve. Your speed increases. You can take on more difficult assignments. You can branch off from the printed page.

You can learn to become better at loving others. Practice the principles of love and grow in your people skills.

4. Love is costly

> *"Greater **love** has no one than this:*
> *to **lay down one's life** for one's friends."*
> JOHN 15:13 (EMPHASIS ADDED)

> *This is how we know what **love** is: Jesus Christ **laid down his life** for us.*
> *And we ought to lay down our lives for our brothers and sisters.*
> 1 JOHN 3:16 (EMPHASIS ADDED)

Jesus *spoke* of His love for His followers. He actively *served* them. But His love went beyond that. He also *sacrificed* His life for them. Those with effective relationships love others with a sacrificial, often costly, love.

Generous sacrifice is a great expression of friendship and love. Love is a matter of giving, not getting. Too often people talk about relationships in terms of what they *get* as opposed to what they *give*. Real love is not selfish; it's sacrificial. It's not taking for me, it's giving to you.

Love is costly. It carries the price tag of time, effort, vulnerability, humility, and self-denial. Laying our lives down for others may not mean that we physically die for them, like Jesus did for us. But it does mean letting ourselves be used up for others. It will cost us. But ultimately it's worth it.

I don't know if it's a true story, but my pastor used to tell a beautiful tale of a little boy whose sister needed a blood transfusion. The doctor explained that she had the same disease the boy had recovered from two years earlier. Her only chance of recovery was a transfusion from someone who had previously conquered the disease. Because the two children had the same rare blood type, the boy was an ideal donor.

"Would you give blood to your sister?" the doctor asked.

The little boy hesitated. His lower lip started to tremble. Then he smiled and sighed, "Sure, for my sister."

Soon the two children were wheeled into the hospital room.

The sick sister was pale and thin. Her brother was stronger and healthy. Neither spoke, but when their eyes met, he grinned at her.

As the nurse inserted the needle, the smile faded from his face. He anxiously watched the blood flow through the tube.

When the ordeal was nearly over, the little boy's quavering voice broke the silence. "Doctor, when do I die?" he gulped. "Will it be much longer?"

Only then did the doctor realize why the little boy had been hesitant at first. He thought that giving his blood to his sister would mean giving up his own life. In a moment he had made the decision to give the blood—because he loved his sister with a costly love.

5. Love is rewarding

Charles Colson was one of President Nixon's cabinet members who went to jail in the Watergate scandal. There he met God and began a marvelous ministry to prisoners.

Years later, a letter came to Colson's Prison Fellowship headquarters. An inmate in New Hampshire was asking the staff to "please pray for Grandma Howell, 'cause she's sick and may be going to die. Nobody has ever loved me like she has. I just wait for her letters, they mean so much."

A few months after that, Prison Fellowship received a letter from Grandma Howell herself, in which she asked Charles Colson to someday speak at her funeral. When Colson wrote back, he discovered she was a ninety-one-year-old woman who kept up correspondence with as many as forty prisoners at a time.

One day Colson got the opportunity to be in her area of Georgia. Looking forward to finally meeting her, he was shocked to find that she lived in one of the dreariest nursing homes in the state. As he entered the soot-covered building, he was sickened by the number of people waiting to die. But when he visited her room, Colson found she was unlike the other residents he had seen. While they radiated death, she radiated life. This tiny, crippled, white-haired grandma lit up as she told Colson of the joy she felt spending her days sharing the love of God with prisoners through her letters. She went to them in the only way a crippled old woman could—by mail. She contacted them and connected with them. And they loved her for it.[1]

Reuben Welch writes, "When I began to love, care for, and become involved with people, I had more life, more tears, more laughter, more meaning, and far greater fun and joy than I ever had before."[2]

What Now?

List the names of ten people in your current sphere of relationships. Prayerfully think of ways you can actively show love to at least five of these people this week.

Notes

1. Adapted from Charles Colson, *Loving God* (Grand Rapids: Zondervan, 1996), 209–216.

2. Reuben Welch, *We Really Do Need Each Other* (Nashville, TN: John T. Benson, 1976), 11.

4

Honor

Honor one another above yourselves.
ROMANS 12:10

"Jesus in Disguise"

Agnes Bojaxhiu spent her adult life serving the poor, sick, orphaned, and dying among the poorest of the poor in the horrific slums of Calcutta, India. When she started an open-air school for slum children, she was joined by volunteer helpers. Financial support began to come in as she loved and cared for people that no one else was prepared to look after.

Later known as Mother Teresa, Agnes was dearly loved the world over. In 1979 she was honored with the Nobel Peace Prize "for work undertaken in the struggle to overcome poverty and distress." Not surprisingly, she refused the conventional ceremonial banquet given to laureates and asked that the funds ($192,000) instead be given to the poor in India.

The secret of Mother Teresa's global impact flowed from the way she saw people. She did not see the people she served as wrapped in filth, filled with disease, disfigured by sores, or covered with flies. She saw something else. When asked how she could love such filthy, stinking, sick, helpless, hopeless people, she simply answered, "Each one of them is Jesus in disguise."[1]

Secret #4
Honor others.

I used to have two colleagues who were similar in many respects but whose lives had vastly different impacts. Both had PhDs. Both were respected professors. Both were committed Christians. Yet one was very popular and loved by his students while the other was. . .let's just say he was not as well loved. The first man led a thriving ministry. The other man's church was dying.

What was the difference?

The way they treated people.

Although this wasn't the entire reason, it summarized the situation clearly. Whenever I saw the first man, he always smiled, always said my name, and always said something affirming to me. I walked away after talking with him feeling valued by him and better about myself. I noticed that he treated everyone this way. He honored people.

My other colleague was not someone you liked to see coming. He usually made a dig, a cut, or a cute comment. He could be belittling, condescending, and patronizing—and often was. He almost never gave a compliment. When I walked away after talking with him, I usually felt depreciated or worn down. He treated everyone this way. He failed to actively honor other people.

Nothing builds a relationship more than the atmosphere of esteem and honor. Nothing erodes it more than a climate of disrespect. When a person breathes an atmosphere of respect and regard, others respond. People respect people who respect them. If you want to have better relationships, learn to honor others.

Honor One Another

> *Honor one another above yourselves.*
> ROMANS 12:10

By the twelfth chapter of Paul's letter to the Romans, he gets very practical. When he gives relational advice, honoring others is central. The Greek word Paul chooses for "honor" speaks of "placing high value on" others. It means "to prefer," "give precedence to," "defer to," and "revere." Paul adds that we are to honor one another *above* ourselves. We are to let others have the credit. The grammar of this verse carries the idea that when we seek to honor others, it is not to make ourselves look good—instead, we are to compete to see who can honor others the most.

Below is a chart that shows the difference between actions that honor others and actions that take advantage of others. See which ones you're already good at and which ones you need to work on.

Actions That Honor Others	Actions That Dishonor Others
Actively try to help others look good even at your own expense	Try to make yourself look good at someone else's expense
Words of appreciation and affirmation	Disapproval, criticism, putdowns
Give credit	Take credit
Take the initiative to clear up misunderstandings	Refuse to act to resolve misunderstandings
Criticize only in private	Criticize in front of others
Ask others for their opinions	Fail to seek the opinions of others
Update people on their status, progress, or anything else that may affect them	Keep people in the dark and purposely withhold information
Impartiality	Favoritism
Give your full attention, active listening	Disinterest
Notice when others need encouragement and give it	Fail to notice the feelings of others, insensitive

The Honor Cycle

Unconditional honor and respect is incredibly powerful in building relationships. When honor is present it will greatly reduce the number of conflicts you experience in your relationships. It will energize your relationships and enhance your friendships.

Jesus said we should treat others as we hope they will treat us.

> *"In everything, do to others what you would have them do to you, for this sums up the Law and the Prophets."*
> MATTHEW 7:12

Honoring others tends to work in a cycle. Relationship expert Dr. Emerson Eggerichs refers to the "Crazy Cycle," in which couples do the same crazy things over and over again with the same negative results. The opposite of that is what I call the Honor Cycle.

The Honor Cycle works like this: if you honor and respect others, the odds increase that they will honor and respect you, and your relationship will begin to spiral upward. No matter where you start from, the relationship can go as high as both people wish *if* both will diligently and consistently do their part. The more both people put into doing their part, the faster it will go.

Yet the converse is also true. If you fail to honor others, they will be less likely to honor you, and you'll be more likely to lapse into the Crazy Cycle.

The beautiful aspect of the Honor Cycle is that you have the power to speed the process. The more often you give others honor and respect, the easier it will be for them to respect you. If you want more respect, give greater honor.

Just as you can speed the process, you also can slow it down or even accelerate it in the wrong direction. If you fail to give others honor and respect, they will not give it in return.

Reaping and Sowing

> *Do not be deceived: God cannot be mocked.*
> *A man reaps what he sows.*
> GALATIANS 6:7

It is called the Law of the Harvest. If a farmer hopes to harvest a crop of wheat, he first must plant some wheat. If he fails to plant anything, he cannot expect to reap anything. If he fails to plant wheat, he will not reap wheat.

The Law of the Harvest extends beyond the farm into the sphere of relationships as well. For example, the next time you eat in a restaurant, treat your waitress with respect. Make her feel like a peer or above. I guarantee she will reciprocate by giving you better service. On the other hand, if treat your waitress as if she is intellectually and socially beneath you, you will notice that the service she provides is probably the bare minimum.

If you want to reap honor in your relationships, start by honoring others. It will usually be reciprocated. If a father treats his son with respect, his son will usually respond with respect. If a pastor honors his flock, they will honor him. If a professor treats her class with respect, they will listen to and respect her.

Esteem Others as Better Than Yourself

We do not know a lot about the first century church at Philippi, but we do know that they had some unity struggles (see Philippians 1:27; 2:1–11; 4:2–5). In the second chapter of his letter to the Philippians, Paul shows the type of persons they need to be in order to glorify God through their relationships.

First, Paul calls them to add to his joy by living in unity, love, and harmony with each other.

> *Fill up and complete my joy by living in harmony and being of the same mind and one in purpose, having the same love, being in full accord and of one harmonious mind and intention.*
> PHILIPPIANS 2:2 AMP

Then Paul tells them *how* to live in harmonious relationships. The secret is very simple, but not necessarily easy—stop being self-centered and start being selfless in your approach to others.

Do nothing from factional motives [through contentiousness, strife, selfishness, or for unworthy ends] or prompted by conceit and empty arrogance. Instead, in the true spirit of humility (lowliness of mind) let each regard the others as better than and superior to himself [thinking more highly of one another than you do of yourselves]. Let each of you esteem and look upon and be concerned for not [merely] his own interests, but also each for the interests of others.

PHILIPPIANS 2:3–4 AMP

In these verses Paul addresses self-centeredness as an obvious relationship killer. Close relationships cannot coexist with self-centeredness, which destroys unity, harmony, and intimacy. In this verse, self-centeredness has three primary expressions: a competitive spirit, a proud heart, and a selfish outlook.

Relationship Killers

1. A competitive spirit

"Do nothing from factional motives [through contentiousness, strife, selfishness, or for unworthy ends]": Overly competitive people always struggle in relationships. They view others as rivals and always seek to "win." They *get angry or sulk in self-pity when they aren't considered* right, first, or best. Selfishly ambitious people can't stand it when others get the credit, get the promotion, or enjoy success, because they wrongly feel as if they've lost out. A competitive spirit does not build relationships. It kills them.

2. A proud heart

"*Do nothing. . .prompted by conceit and empty arrogance*": Proud people are arrogant and boastful. They have an insatiable thirst for attention and validation. Self-centered people end up with an excessively high or inflated view of themselves. They think of themselves as superior to others and expect to be served. Looking down on others from a supposed position of superiority kills relationships.

3. A selfish outlook

"*Let each of you esteem and look upon and be concerned for not [merely] his own interests*": Selfish people are obsessively focused on themselves. They think and talk so much about themselves, their well-being, their comfort, their activities, their feelings, their problems, and their opinions that they totally overlook the true needs of others. Instead of building unity, intimacy, and harmony, selfishness destroys it.

Relationship Builders

Paul not only points out the relationship killers—he also gives four powerful relationship builders.

1. A humble spirit

"*In the true spirit of humility (lowliness of mind)*": True humility builds relationships. True humility is not so much thinking negatively of yourself as it is thinking accurately about yourself and others, realizing that we are all recipients of God's unmerited grace and unconditional mercy. Everything good about any of us is by the gracious gift of God. True humility is not so much thinking poorly of yourself as it is thinking so much about others that you are not thinking much about yourself at all.

2. An honoring attitude

"Let each regard the others as better than and superior to himself [thinking more highly of one another than you do of yourselves]": Too often we think too highly of ourselves by focusing on negative things about others and overlooking the negative things about ourselves. An honoring attitude actively regards and mentions the positive things about others. An honoring attitude seeks the good of others, even when it comes at our own expense.

3. A servant approach

"Let each of you esteem and look upon and be concerned for not [merely] his own interests, but also each for the interests of others": Nothing hurts a relationship like one person feeling as if they've been used by another to get ahead. Paul advises putting oneself aside in order to help others get ahead.

4. An others-oriented mind-set

"Let each of you esteem and look upon and be concerned for not [merely] his own interests, but also each for the interests of others": An others-oriented spirit seeks to promote others ahead of ourselves. It is letting go of the obsession to get our own advantage and forgetting ourselves to help others get ahead. Our heartbeat becomes meeting the needs of others and helping *them* succeed. It is saying, "I'm here to serve you and help you get where you want to go."

The Accompanist

Tim is one of the finest young pianists in the country. He is an incredible musician with natural gifts and genius honed through years of diligent practice. He enjoys perfect pitch and flawless tonal memory. Everyone loves him for his active humility, especially those students he accompanies on the piano. He is noted for the encouraging words he offers to everyone he plays for.

During a performance, Tim carefully works his magic to play in such a way as to make the young soloists sound their very best. He lowers his volume to show off the singer's strengths and raises it at exactly the right moment to hide their weaknesses. His facial expressions show his abundant joy in their success. His body language focuses all of the attention on the vocalist when the applause of the crowd celebrates the pair for the job they have just completed. In this way, Tim honors others and has built many strong relationships as a result.

"Make Me Feel Important"

Mary Kay Ash retired in her mid-forties to write a book to help women in business. The book turned into a business plan for her ideal company. After her husband died, she launched her new business with a five thousand dollar investment. Founded on the golden rule, her cosmetics company blossomed. She advocated "praising people to success," and her slogan, "God first, family second, career third," expressed her insistence that the women in her company keep their lives in balance. She wrote three books that all became bestsellers.

Much of Mary Kay's success in life and business was based on her commitment to honor others. She observed, "Everyone has an invisible sign hanging from their neck saying, 'Make me feel important.' Never forget this message when working with people."[2] She also shrewdly noted, "There are two things that people want more than sex and money—recognition and praise."[3]

"Made in My Image"

In order to glorify God and to be effective, honoring others has to be more than a technique. It must be a core value. We must develop the lifestyle of discerning and expressing the value of other human beings. We must assign value and high worth to others by viewing them as God does: *priceless*. John Ortberg writes, "Every human being carries [a] sticker from God: 'Made in my image; worth the life of my Son. My prized possession whose value is beyond calculation.'"[4]

"Just to Be on the Safe Side"

The story is told of a poor traveler who was astounded by the treatment he received at a particular monastery. He was served a lavish meal, escorted to the finest room, and given a new set of clothes. As he left, he commented to the abbot about how extremely well he had been treated.

"We treat our guests as if they are angels," the abbot said, "just to be on the safe side."

What Now?

Let me offer some suggestions for how you can practically honor others:

- See everyone as made in God's image and someone Jesus died for.
- Say "thank you" often.
- Affirm and encourage others.
- Return calls, texts, and e-mails promptly.
- Don't keep others waiting.
- Stand up when someone enters the room.
- Call if you are running late.
- Don't correct adults in front of others.
- Let your subordinates shine.
- Give the credit away.
- Keep the promises you make.
- Treat subordinates as equals.
- Do not pull rank on someone.
- Keep confidences sacred.
- Do not use information shared in confidence against that person.
- See others as wearing a sign that reads, "Make me feel important."
- Only speak negatively of ideas or policies, not people.
- Never criticize someone else's children.

- Do not milk a friend for information.
- Never conspire with others against a friend.
- Do not let friends get blindsided by their weaknesses.
- Clarify issues with truth.
- Be sensitive with practical jokes.
- Never flatter.
- Don't get involved in others' affairs unless invited.
- Compliment deeds done well.
- Clean up after yourself.
- Use good manners.
- Don't compete, complete.
- Never climb over someone to get ahead.
- Lend a hand.
- Laugh *with* others, but only laugh *at* yourself.
- Honor others by seeing them as "Jesus in disguise."

Notes

1. Mother Teresa, www.brainyquote.com/quotes/authors/m/mother_teresa_2.html.

2. Mary Kay Ash, www. quotationsbook.com/quote/31858.

3. Mary Kay Ash, http://www.brainyquote.com/quotes/quotes m/marykayash148279.html.

4. Ortberg, *Everybody's Normal*, 205.

5

Serve

"Wash one another's feet."
John 13:14

Serve one another humbly in love.
Galatians 5:13

"What Was He Doing Now?"

It had to be one of the oddest and most awkward moments they had ever experienced. Of course, since the disciples had been following Jesus, the odd and awkward moments were surprisingly frequent. He was so different from anyone they had ever known. And now here it was the night of the Passover feast, and He did it again.

What did Jesus do this time? Walk on water? Raise the dead? Miraculously feed thousands? No. He did not perform a miracle that revealed His power as God. Instead He took the opportunity to reveal His heart as a friend.

The scene occurred in first-century Jerusalem. Most roads were made of dirt and were covered with a thick layer of dust. It was customary for hosts to provide a slave at the door to wash the feet of guests as they arrived. The servant would kneel with a pitcher of water, a basin, and a towel. If the host could not afford a slave, he or one of the early arriving guests would take upon himself the role of servant and wash the feet of those who came. What is interesting in this story is that none of the disciples had volunteered for the task of servant. They left that up to someone else.

That "someone else" was Jesus.

We should understand that the disciples did not sit on chairs during dinner—rather, they reclined around a low table. In such a setting it was common to have someone else's feet near your face, so this task of washing feet was vital to the success and pleasure of the meal.

Jesus, their rabbi, must have embarrassed them all when He began to wash their feet. Chuck Swindoll writes, "Serving and giving don't come naturally. *Living an unselfish life is an art.*"[1] In John 13 we see Jesus, the master artist of unselfishness in action. We see a portrait of service.

Secret #5
Loving service.

The Portrait of a Servant

*It was just before the Passover Festival. **Jesus knew** that the hour had come for him to leave this world and go to the Father. Having loved his own who were in the world, he loved them to the end. The evening meal was in progress, and the devil had already prompted Judas, the son of Simon Iscariot, to betray Jesus. **Jesus knew** that the Father had put all things under his power, and that he had come from God and was returning to God.*

JOHN 13:1–3 (EMPHASIS ADDED)

Twice in this section we read that "Jesus knew." Jesus knew who He was. Jesus knew where He was going. Jesus knew where He came from. He was secure and confident in His identity. This deep sense of spiritual security and personal confidence was His platform for love and service.

I have found that my ability to be a loving servant to others flows out of having the right attitudes about myself. When I get a real grip on how much God loves me, I am better able to love and serve others.

1. Servants have nothing to prove

When Jesus got up to serve, He didn't announce it. He just did it. Jesus didn't have to prove Himself. When we're caught up in proving ourselves, we fail to see the real needs of others.

Sometimes, like when our kids ask us tough questions, we think we have to have all the answers. Sometimes we act as if we live on a pedestal. We know we're not perfect, but rather than admit it, we try to cover it up. Jesus never acted that way. His attitude was that He had nothing to prove. It was like He said, "I'm not doing this to prove that I'm a good person or to show that I'm better than you—but simply because I love you and you need it."

2. Servants have nothing to lose

In those days rabbis held positions of great esteem, especially over their disciples. You would never expect a rabbi to take the role of servant and wash feet. That would ruin his reputation. But Jesus wasn't hung up on His reputation or position.

Jesus had already given up all the glories of heaven to come to earth and be a man. He laid aside His divine attributes and took the role of servant. He had already given up much and knew that He would soon give up even more. He had come to die.

Jesus clearly had nothing to lose. He wasn't worried about His reputation. He was simply concerned about doing what needed to be done. It didn't matter that He was the rabbi, the disciples' master. It only mattered that He loved them and they needed their feet washed.

3. Servants have nothing to hide

Jesus was a man of integrity. There were no skeletons in His closet. He had no dirty laundry. He could serve greatly because He lived rightly. He had nothing to hide, nothing to lose, and nothing to prove. He had all the attitudes of a loving servant.

I find that my own selfish attitude often hamstrings my ability to serve. Selfishness leads me to hide, to try to prove something, to hang on when I need to let go and serve.

4. Servants express their love

Jesus expressed His love for His disciples through His service to them. Look back through this passage again and note the actions Jesus took to express His love:

> Having **loved** his own who were in the world, he loved them to the end. The evening meal was in progress, and the devil had already prompted Judas, the son of Simon Iscariot, to betray Jesus. Jesus knew that the Father had put all things under his power, and that he had come from God and was returning to God; so he **got up** from the meal, **took off** his outer clothing, and **wrapped** a towel around his waist. After that, he **poured** water into a basin and **began to wash** his disciples' feet, **drying** them with the towel that was wrapped around him.
>
> JOHN 13:1–5 (EMPHASIS ADDED)

Love is always expressed. It goes beyond fond thoughts to obvious expressions. The Bible says that Jesus "loved his own." Then it describes how He showed them the full extent of His love by serving them. If you love other people, your life should surely show it.

Expressing our love may not come easily. We've all heard about the middle aged couple who came in for marriage counseling. The counselor asked the wife to explain the problem and she said, "He does not love me." The counselor looked at the man and asked if it was true. The man said, "No, that's not true."

The counselor turned to the woman and asked her why she thought her husband didn't love her. She said, "Because he never tells me he loves me."

The husband shook his head in disgust, "Woman, I told you I loved you when I married you and that if I ever changed my mind I'd let you know."

Love that is unexpressed is love that is unrecognized. Jesus' love was easily recognized because it was often expressed.

5. Servants take action

By its very nature, service is active. Jesus didn't just sit around saying, "I love you." He showed it by His actions. He *got up*, *took off*, *wrapped*, *poured*, *washed*, and *dried*. He met the need at hand. Real love is always active. It cannot sit still when there is a need to be met.

I read an interesting statistic the other day. Only 49 percent of the women in America said that if they had it to do over again, they would marry the same man. Yet of the women whose husbands helped around the house, 82 percent said they'd marry the same man again. Why is that the case? Because love is actively expressed.

What makes the events recorded in John 13 so memorable and

startling is that what Jesus did was entirely out of character for a rabbi in that day. Rabbis were to be served. They were not about humbling themselves; they were into exalting themselves. That was the way it was done. Yet Jesus stood convention on its ear and lowered Himself to serve and to meet needs.

I find that my greatest obstacle in being a loving servant is. . .*me*. *I'm* always in the way. *I'm* too busy. *I'm* too tired. *I'm* too focused on *myself* and *my* situation to see the needs of others, especially those closest to me. Jesus showed us something most of us need to see—the art of unselfish living. Servants are willing to brush aside *self* in order to see what someone else needs and to act to meet that need.

Mother Teresa personified love through active service as she cared for the least of the least in the slums of Calcutta. In speaking of serving lowly people she said, "We can do no great things; only small things with great love."[2] When asked why she could serve so tirelessly she replied, "Love cannot remain by itself—it has no meaning. Love has to be put into action, and that action is service."[3]

The Call to Servanthood

As we mentioned in chapter four, the church at Philippi was divided. To help the Philippians understand how to experience relationships with unity, harmony, and spiritual intimacy, Paul pointed back to the example of Jesus.

> *In your relationships with one another, have the same mindset as Christ Jesus: Who, being in very nature God, did not consider equality with God something to be used to his own advantage; rather, he made himself nothing by taking the very nature of a servant, being made in human likeness. And being found in appearance as a man, he humbled himself by becoming obedient to death—even death on a cross!*
>
> PHILIPPIANS 2:5–8

In this passage of scripture, Paul not only shows us that Jesus was a servant but also how *we* can become servants by following His example.

1. Do not cling to your rights

Philippians 2:6 states that Jesus, who had equal status with God, didn't cling to the advantages of that status. If anyone had rights, Jesus did. If anyone laid down His rights to serve others, Jesus did. He had the right, as God, to have everyone serve Him.

We must get past the notion that we somehow deserve to have

others serve us. We must lay aside the "right" to be served. We must stop *expecting* to be served. *We* need to be the ones who serve.

2. Set aside your privileges

Philippians 2:7 says that Jesus set aside the privileges of deity and took on the status of a slave by becoming human. What a huge step down—from the lofty position of the infinite, almighty God to that of lowly human!

What staggers me most is that Jesus came to earth as a member of a lowly nation in servitude to the Roman Empire. I think if I were God and decided to become human in the first century, I'd at least make myself the emperor of Rome. But that's not what Jesus did.

If I were God and chose to come to earth as a Jew, I'd be the powerful high priest in Jerusalem. Not Jesus. He was the son of a Nazareth carpenter in lowly Galilee.

If I were God and chose to become human, I'd at least come as an adult. Not Jesus. He came as a helpless newborn.

If I were God and chose to become a human baby, I'd be born somewhere clean and nice, surrounded by a huge, loving family. Not Jesus. He was born in a barn surrounded by cows and sheep.

The message to us is that true service is not selective. Once we adopt the attitude of a servant, no privilege is sacred. We will lay aside our perceived privileges and go to whatever point is necessary to meet the need. Nothing is beneath us. Nothing is too low for us to do in order to serve.

3. Live a humble, selfless, obedient lifestyle

Philippians 2:8 tells us that Jesus did not take the servant approach for a brief period and then resume His rights and privileges as God when the serving became uncomfortable. No! He willingly abased and humbled Himself still further and carried His obedience to the extreme of death—and the worst kind of death imaginable to a Jew: crucifixion.

The application for us is that service is not a temporary activity we do to appease a guilty conscience or to make ourselves look better. It is a lifestyle we live out every day of our lives.

Jesus also did not take the servant mind-set based on how others received it. Jesus would have gone to the cross even if no one responded, because He was doing more than an act of service. He was obeying His Father's will.

Ultimately we serve to please God, whether our service is received by the person being served or not. We do it anyway, because being a servant is who we are and such an approach pleases God. In fact, as Jesus modeled servanthood for us, God the Father was so pleased that He gave Jesus the highest position possible.

Therefore God exalted him to the highest place and gave him the name that is above every name, that at the name of Jesus ever knee should bow, in heaven and on earth and under the earth, and every tongue acknowledge that Jesus Christ is Lord, to the glory of God the Father.
PHILIPPIANS 2:9–11

God exalted and blessed Jesus after—and because—Jesus chose to be a servant. God will ultimately honor us and bless our relationships as we truly live as servants to others.

What Now?

How do you stack up as a servant? Do you serve confidently as one who has nothing to hide, nothing to lose, and nothing to prove? Do you express your love and take action? Do you lay aside your rights and privileges in order to meet the needs of others? Are you becoming a servant by lifestyle or do you merely do occasional acts of service?

Notes

1. Charles R. Swindoll, *Improving Your Serve* (Nashville: W, 1981), 12, emphasis added.

2. Mother Teresa, www.brainyquote.com/quotes/authors/m/mother_teresa_2 .html.

3. Ibid.

6

Forgive

In his 1984 book *Forgive and Forget,* Lewis Smedes writes,

Someone hurt you, maybe yesterday, maybe a lifetime ago, but you cannot forget it. You did not deserve the hurt. It went deep—deep enough to lodge itself not only in your memory, but also in your heart. And it keeps on hurting you now. You are not alone. We all muddle through a world in which even well-meaning people hurt each other. [1]

When we open up our souls to another person, when we invest ourselves in deep personal relationships, we take a risk. We could always get hurt. The more we expose ourselves, the greater the potential pain. No one can hurt us like someone we've trusted with our heart. No one.

Deep hurts from past relationships can poison and pollute our present attempts at bettering our relationships. These unhealed wounds fester and spread until they steal our joy, pilfer our peace, rob our intimacy with God, and shortchange our possibilities of close relationships. Each old hurt becomes like a bar locking our souls into a prison of bitterness. They become shackles holding us back and dragging us down.

But it doesn't have to be that way.

Jesus provided a new means for dealing with old wounds.

It's called forgiveness.

Forgiveness is the Christian key of a liberated soul. It is also a significant secret to better relationships.

Secret #6
Forgive.

How Many Times Shall I Forgive?

In many ways Peter was the most human of the disciples. He had a knack for speaking his mind and putting his foot in his mouth. Maybe that's why we like him so much.

Thank God he did! Because Peter had the courage (or stupidity) to say what the rest of us might have been thinking, his interactions with the Lord provided many insights into how to really follow Jesus.

One day Peter approached Jesus with a question that had been bugging him. Someone close to Peter must have hurt him—and not just once, but several times. Peter was wrestling with the reasons for, the extent of, and the limits to forgiveness. So he asked Jesus about it.

> *Then Peter came to Jesus and asked, "Lord, how many times shall I forgive my brother or sister who sins against me? Up to seven times?"*
> MATTHEW 18:21

Peter probably thought Jesus would commend him. After all, the rabbis usually taught that the obligation to forgive stopped after *three* times. Peter had doubled that and added one more on top. But Jesus came to provide a life that far excelled that of the rabbis.

> *Jesus answered, "I tell you, not seven times, but seventy-seven times."*
> MATTHEW 18:22

Seventy-seven times! Jesus topped Peter's magnanimity by

eleven times! What is He saying?

The point is not that Peter needed to count every time a particular person offended him then at number seventy-eight let him have it. Jesus is using an extreme number to say that forgiveness is to be a lifestyle.

John Ortberg points out that Jesus was also reversing the law of revenge instituted by the Bible character Lamech.[2] Lamech was a grandson of Cain and a great-grandson of Adam. The Bible says little else about him, but it does record the legacy of revenge he left his wives and sons.

> *Lamech said to his wives, "Adah and Zillah, listen to me; wives of*
> *Lamech, hear my words. I have killed a man for wounding me,*
> *a young man for injuring me. If Cain is avenged seven times,*
> *then Lamech seventy-seven times."*
>
> GENESIS 4:23–24

Lamech killed a man who wounded him and boasted that he would seek revenge seventy-seven times against anyone who hurt him. According to Lamech's law of revenge, if anyone hurts me, I will hurt him in return and make him pay far worse than I received.

Peter would have known Lamech's law of revenge, so Jesus stood it on its ear. If Lamech's law of revenge was to inflict vengeance seventy-seven times worse than received, then Jesus' law of forgiveness was to *forgive* hurt seventy-seven times.

The Story of Forgiveness Extended

As a master teacher, Jesus always seized teachable moments and told stories to drive home His points. We call these stories parables. On this occasion Jesus told a parable about the nature of forgiveness.

> *"Therefore, the kingdom of heaven is like a king who wanted to settle accounts with his servants. As he began the settlement, a man who owed him ten thousand bags of gold was brought to him. Since he was not able to pay, the master ordered that he and his wife and his children and all that he had be sold to repay the debt."*
>
> MATTHEW 18:23–25

A king had his books audited and discovered an embezzler. The embezzler owed the king an astronomical amount of money. The term "ten thousand" used in a plural sense was the largest number in the language of Jesus' day. It was equivalent to saying the man owed the king *zillions* of dollars. It is more money than could be imagined and certainly more than he could ever repay.

The punishment for such an offense was debtor's prison. Debtors and their families would be enslaved to work off their debt. A male slave like this servant would fetch about two thousand dollars. His wife and children would bring only a fraction of that amount. Yet he owed "ten thousand bags of gold." The debt would never be paid in his lifetime. His descendants could be slaves for generations.

This man was in big trouble. There was no chapter 11 bankruptcy in his day. There was no Mega Millions lottery he could try. He had nothing else to lose.

So he begged.

> *"At this the servant fell on his knees before him.*
> *'Be patient with me,' he begged, 'and I will pay back everything.'"*
> MATTHEW 18:26

No one expected what happened next.

> *"The servant's master took pity on him,*
> *canceled the debt and let him go."*
> MATTHEW 18:27

When Jesus told this story, no one listening would have expected this turn of events. It just wasn't done, ever. Kings always made debtors pay what they owed. But this king was different. He chose to live by the law of forgiveness.

No slavery. No prison.

The man did not have to pay back anything!

The entire debt was erased.

The king absorbed it all.

The Story of Forgiveness Denied

Unfortunately the story doesn't end there. The newly forgiven debtor happened to have a debtor of his own.

> *"But when that servant went out, he found one of his fellow servants who owed him a hundred silver coins. He grabbed him and began to choke him. 'Pay back what you owe me!' he demanded. His fellow servant fell to his knees and begged him, 'Be patient with me, and I will pay it back.' But he refused. Instead, he went off and had the man thrown into prison until he could pay the debt."*
> MATTHEW 18:28–30

After this man had received the astounding unconditional cancellation of his monumental debt, you would fully expect him to forgive the man who owed him less than a hundred coins. But he didn't. He didn't consider the poor man who could not repay. He only saw a handful of coins. So he refused to take the forgiveness he had received and extend it to another.

And the king found out. This is the same king who had just canceled the man's massive debt. He was not happy.

> *"When the other servants saw what had happened, they were outraged and went and told their master everything that had happened. Then the master called the servant in. 'You wicked servant,' he said,*

'I canceled all that debt of yours because you begged me to. Shouldn't you have had mercy on your fellow servant just as I had on you?' In anger his master handed him over to the jailers to be tortured, until he should pay back all he owed."

MATTHEW 18:31–34

The Story Behind the Story

Jesus told this story to show us a bigger story called *redemption*. The reality is that each of us owes the King of the universe, God, a gargantuan debt racked up by our sin. It is a debt we can never repay. It is a debt that condemns us to an eternal prison of guilt and shame.

Yet when we come to the King seeking mercy, He graciously extends forgiveness to us. He cancels our debt fully and completely. The King is able to do this because His Son already paid the debt for us.

Such costly forgiveness should prompt us to forgive others the much smaller debts owed to us because of offenses they may have caused. John Ortberg writes, "What Jesus does at infinite cost, he invites us to do as well, though at a much lesser expense."[3]

This story further tells us that failing to forgive will ultimately hurt us more than it hurts the other person. It locks us into a dungeon of torture and a prison of bitterness.

Although the bars, chains, and torture chambers of this prison aren't visible, they are every bit as real. When we harbor bitterness in our hearts toward someone else, we unwittingly become a prisoner to them. Just the mention of their name can flood our minds with powerful and ugly thoughts. Seeing the person elevates our heart rate and blood pressure. Hearing their voice can make us wince and cringe. Even when they are not even thinking about us, we cannot get them out of our minds. We become their prisoner, and our bitterness toward them tortures us.

There is only one way out of the horrible prison of harbored hurts. Only one key turns the lock of freedom from the jail cell of resentment: forgiveness.

Failure to Forgive Is Costly

Lack of forgiveness is devastatingly powerful. It produces the awful fruit of resentment, bitterness, anger, hatred, strife, and jealousy. When we have unresolved hurts, we will find ourselves responding with insults, attacks, broken relationships, betrayal, and distance from God. Lack of forgiveness rips apart families, divides marriages, splits churches, and poisons friendships.

Recent studies have found that learning to forgive brings wonderful physical healing and power—and that there is great danger in withholding forgiveness. "Carrying around a load of bitterness and anger at how unfairly you were treated is very toxic," says Dr. Fred Luskin, director of Stanford University's Forgiveness

Project. His researchers found that letting go of a grudge can slash one's stress level up to 50 percent. Volunteers in the study showed improvements in energy, mood, sleep quality, and overall physical vitality. Another study has shown that giving up grudges can reduce chronic back pain. Yet another experiment found that practicing forgiveness limited relapses among women battling substance abuse.

Physically, anger and resentment produce a steady stream of stress hormones, which then turn into toxins. According to Dr. Bruce McEwen, director of the neurological lab at Rockefeller University in New York City, these toxins wear down the brain, leading to cell atrophy and memory loss. Stress also raises blood sugar, hardens arteries, and leads to heart disease. On the other hand, forgiveness stops these hormones from flowing.

In a separate study of thirty-six men who had coronary heart disease and a history of painful hurts, half were given forgiveness training and half were not. The ones who forgave showed greater blood flow to their hearts.

Forgiveness is costly. But there is only one thing that costs more.

Unforgiveness.

Forgiveness Is Not. . .

John Ortberg and Lewis Smedes helped me clarify exactly what forgiveness is and what it is not. Several of the ideas below are adapted from their observations.[4]

1. Forgiveness is not the same thing as excusing

When an action is excusable, it does not require forgiveness.

2. Forgiveness is not tolerating sin

It is not being a doormat. In a television message titled "Five Things Everyone Should Know about Forgiving," Lewis Smedes taught, "Forgive those who wrong you, but do not tolerate their wrongdoing. Forgive them and tell them what Jesus told the people that He forgave: 'You are forgiven for what you did, but stop it, don't do it again.'"[5]

3. Forgiveness is not forgetting

It is biologically impossible to forget severe hurts. You cannot just erase them from your memory. When the Bible says that God "forgets our sins," it means that His present treatment of us is not tainted by our past offenses. John Ortberg writes, "Forgiving is what's required precisely when we *can't* forget."[6]

4. Forgiveness is not foolishness

If someone cheats you in a business deal, you are to forgive them, but you are not required to do business with them again. If you have been abused by someone who has no interest in changing, you should forgive them but not move back in with them. Forgiveness is something I can choose to extend even if the other person never asks for it or doesn't deserve it.

5. Forgiveness is not waiting until other people say they're sorry

If you wait for some people to say they're sorry, you may wait forever. As Lewis Smedes says, "Why put your happiness in the hands of the person who made you unhappy in the first place? Forgive and let the other person do what he wants. Heal yourself."[7]

Forgiveness Is. . .

1. Forgiveness is canceling the debt

When people hurt us, they owe us. Forgiveness recognizes the debt they owe and chooses to release them from it.

2. Forgiveness is setting yourself free

People who hold grudges find that very soon, the grudge holds them. Forgiveness frees us from resentment. Lewis Smedes writes, "The first person who gets the benefit of forgiving is always the person who does the forgiving. When you forgive a person who wronged you, you set a prisoner free, and then you discover that the prisoner you set free is you. . . . When you forgive, you heal the hurts you never should have felt in the first place."[8]

3. Forgiveness is giving up the right to get even

We tend to keep score of hurts. Forgiveness is choosing not to keep score, not to pay back, not to get even. Forgiveness is suspending the law of revenge.

4. Forgiveness is looking past the hurt to the person

Hurting people usually hurt people. Bitterness can only see the hurt. Forgiveness sees the loneliness, brokenness, weakness, self-centeredness, or blind spot of the one who hurt you.

Paul advised the Ephesians to put off bitterness by putting on sensitivity:

> *Get rid of all bitterness, rage and anger, brawling and slander,*
> *along with every form of malice. Be kind and compassionate to one*
> *another, forgiving each other, just as in Christ God forgave you.*
> EPHESIANS 4:31–32

5. Forgiveness is making four promises

Ken Sande of Peacemaker Ministries writes, "We must release the person who has wronged us from the penalty of being separated from us. We must not hold wrongs against others, not think about the wrongs, and not punish others for them."[9] Sande is an attorney who grew disillusioned with the way the legal system settled lawsuits but destroyed relationships. He studied everything the Bible said about peacemaking and found that real forgiveness may be described as a decision to make four promises:

a. "I will not dwell on this incident."
b. "I will not bring up this incident again and use it against you."
c. "I will not talk to others about this incident."
d. "I will not let this incident stand between us or hinder our personal relationship."[10]

6. Forgiveness is ultimately wishing the other person well
It is reaching a place where you no longer wish the worst for the person who hurt you. You hope good things for them.

7. Forgiveness is something that usually takes some time
When the person was trusted, when the hurt went deep, and when the act was unfair, forgiveness takes time. You will not wish that person well right away. Be patient with yourself. Make the first step. It will get you going and once on the way, you will never want to go back.

8. Forgiveness is walking in step with God

Paul told the Colossians that they were to "bear with each other and forgive one another if any of you has a grievance against someone. Forgive *as the Lord forgave you*" (Colossians 3:13, emphasis added). The challenge of forgiveness is learning to treat others as God has treated us.

9. Forgiveness is impossible without faith

Obviously, no one has the capacity to wish good upon someone who has deeply hurt them. I love Luke's Gospel where he records an instance of Jesus teaching on the radical challenge of forgiveness. He tells them, "Even if they sin against you seven times in a day and seven times come back to you saying 'I repent,' you must forgive them" (Luke 17:4).

Their response is priceless: "The apostles said to the Lord, *'Increase our faith!'*" (Luke 17:5, emphasis added).

What Now?

Odds are good that someone has essentially taken you prisoner because you have not forgiven their offense. Life is too short to be shackled with the ball and chain of an unforgiving heart. Our response to an offense determines our future. Many wonderful opportunities await us when we take the way of escape from the dungeon of resentment.

Picture those who need your forgiveness with their offenses clearly in your mind. Make the choice Jesus made. Choose to begin the process of forgiving.

Notes

1. Lewis B. Smedes, *Forgive and Forget* (New York: 1984, Harper & Row), 11.

2. Ortberg, *Everybody's Normal*, 151–152.

3. Ibid., 156–157.

4. These thoughts on forgiveness are adapted from John Ortberg, *Everybody's Normal Till You Get to Know Them* (Grand Rapids: Zondervan, 2003), 157, and Lewis Smedes, "Five Things Everyone Should Know about Forgiving," *30 Good Minutes*, program #4101, October 5, 1997; http://www.csec.org/csec/sermon/smedes_4101.htm. John Ortberg notes that "forgiving is not the same thing as *excusing*. . . . Forgiving does not mean tolerating bad behavior. . . . Forgiving is not *forgetting*. . . . Forgiving is not the same thing as *reconciling*."

5. Smedes, "Five Things."

6. Ortberg, *Everybody's Normal*, 157. Italics in original.

7. Smedes, "Five Things."

8. Ibid.

9. Ken Sande, *The Peacemaker* (Grand Rapids: Baker, 1991), 209.

10. Ibid.

7

Be Honest

Therefore confess your sins to each other.
JAMES 5:16

"I love you guys."

This was the intimacy-celebrating sentiment expressed by a pack of men who had spent a Saturday morning together. We had eaten breakfast together, sang a few songs, laughed at some bad jokes, and studied scripture. These men had done similar things before with little impact. . .but this day was different.

We had also spent a considerable amount of time confessing our fears and sins to each other and praying for one another. Men shared their fears about losing their jobs. Guys wept over pornography addictions. A surprising number had opened up about being angry and harsh with their wives and children. A couple of men spoke of the guilt they felt over gambling.

It was messy but good. God was obviously there. Honesty had paved the way to intimacy. Men who had come together as little more than strangers were heartily hugging each other and pounding one another on the back. They even started calling other guys "Brother" and actually meant it.

After that day, things were different. Small handfuls of men began meeting weekly for breakfast, Bible study, and accountability. Many commented that they felt as if they were *living* their Christianity for the first time.

That was fifteen years ago. Since then, I have seen the scenario reenacted dozens of times with other groups of men. I have seen it happen at men's retreats and youth retreats, in seminary classrooms, and in home Bible studies. Honesty is the forgotten key to intimacy and a secret to better relationships.

Secret #7
Sincere confession and genuine authenticity.

Intimacy Enjoyed

You know the story. In the beginning, God created the heavens and the earth, the plants and the animals, and man. God surveyed His work and declared it very good (Genesis 1:31). But unlike each of the animals, Adam did not have a corresponding companion. So God took one of Adam's ribs and created a woman.

Adam was no longer alone. He and Eve shared a deep level of intimacy as they were "both naked, and they felt no shame" (Genesis 2:25). Both experienced the joy of fully knowing and being known. They relished the image of God they saw in each other. Fear, shame, guilt, and hiding were absolutely foreign to both of them. All they knew was that they were completely known and unconditionally accepted.

Intimacy Lost

You also know the rest of the story. Theologians call it the Fall. The sweet goodness of the universe crashed. The man and the woman whom God had created disobeyed Him. Sin invaded the world. Depravity invaded mankind. And intimacy vanished.

> *Then **the eyes of both of them were opened**, and they realized they were naked; so they sewed fig leaves together and made coverings for themselves.*
> GENESIS 3:7 (EMPHASIS ADDED)

Their eyes were "opened." This is what they had hoped for when they ate the forbidden fruit. But the dream turned into a nightmare. The serpent had betrayed them!

Before, when they looked at each other, they saw the beauty

of the image of God shining through the other. But now, instead of seeing their best friend, they saw a stranger. Instead of being joyously "other conscious," they now were shamefully self-conscious. Instead of feeling fully known and securely loved, they felt guilt and grief.

They not only saw each other, but they saw themselves. . .as naked and ashamed. So they tried to hide from each other behind fig leaves. And the hiding did not stop there.

> *Then the man and his wife heard the sound of the LORD God*
> *as he was walking in the garden in the cool of the day,*
> *and **they hid from the LORD God** among the trees of the garden.*
> GENESIS 3:8 (EMPHASIS ADDED)

Since the moment of his creation, Adam had always looked forward to the sound of God walking in the garden. But this time it was different. Foreign and ugly feelings washed over him—guilt, shame, fear. So instead of running to God, he ran from Him and hid, like a bad little boy.

> *But the LORD God called to the man, "Where are you?"*
> GENESIS 3:9

This is an interesting question. Why did God ask Adam where he was? Being omniscient and omnipresent, God already knew

Adam's exact location. As John Ortberg keenly observes, "This question is not about geographical location. It is not really a request for information. . . . It is an invitation. God allows Adam to hide. God offers him the opportunity to reveal himself."[1]

> *He [Adam] answered, "I heard you in the garden,*
> *and **I was afraid** because **I was naked; so I hid**."*
> *And he [God] said, "Who told you that you were naked?*
> *Have you eaten from the tree that I commanded you not to eat from?"*
> *The man said, "**The woman you put here with me—***
> *she gave me some fruit from the tree, and I ate it."*
> Genesis 3:10–12 (emphasis added)

Disobedience quickly left a depressing trail. Immediately Adam expressed terror ("I was afraid"); experienced humiliation ("because I was naked"); practiced hiding ("so I hid"); and began blaming ("the woman you put here"). These results—fear, shame, hiding, and blaming—are the same things that sabotage our own efforts at intimacy.

How to Sabotage Intimacy

1. Fear

This is an astounding statement: Before the Fall, there was no fear—no *need* for fear. After the Fall, fear breeds confusion. On one hand we crave intimacy, and on the other we're afraid of it. We're afraid others will see our flaws, weaknesses, and insecurities. We're afraid if others really knew us, they would reject us. We feel like fakes and frauds in a world that seems to have it all together.

2. Shame

Initially Adam and Eve's nakedness was innocent—they were naked, but they felt no shame (Genesis 2:25). But now their nakedness was stained by sin. Now they were naked *and* ashamed. Unlike true guilt, which says, "I have *done* something bad," shame says, "I *am* bad." Shame leaves us feeling cheap and unworthy of love and respect. Guilt is specific. Shame is general. Guilt can have good results in that it drives us to repentance. Shame has no good outcomes.

3. Hiding

Hiding is a curse. It is the result of fear and shame. We hide to keep from being exposed and rejected. We hide to keep from being hurt. We may hide by withdrawing from relationships entirely, but most of us use "fig leaves." Common fig leaves include busyness, humor, shallow conversation, supposed intelligence, or spirituality.

4. Blaming

When we're exposed, as inevitably we are, we try to protect ourselves by shifting the focus from our weakness to someone else's.

Poisoning the Well

As a seminary professor, I train future pastors. One of the courses we recently developed is called Ministry Matters. In it we help potential pastors prepare to face the things that knock people out of vocational ministry. We deal with issues such as the call to vocational ministry, the calling to a specific church, stress, boundaries, burnout, finances, marriage, recreation, people skills, conflict resolution, leadership, and intimacy issues.

As I prepared to write the course curriculum, I was initially surprised at the importance of intimacy in ministerial longevity. But the more I studied, the clearer it became: mishandled intimacy issues not only wreck relationships, they wreck people, including pastors and churches.

Michael Todd Wilson and Brad Hoffmann, in their helpful book *Preventing Ministry Failure*, point out that, "When we reject intimacy with God and like-minded believers, our need for it doesn't go away. It merely goes underground."[2] They explain that our innate God-given desire for intimacy is like radioactive material. When used properly, it generates great power to bless. When buried underground, it leaks out, polluting its surroundings and hurting people. Our yearning for intimacy, when handled properly, provides a full life of vibrant relationships. Burying it eventually contaminates every aspect of our lives.

Wilson and Hoffmann identify more than a dozen indicators of living with a lack of human intimacy. They also give some common, yet inadequate, substitutions for true intimacy. Read through these lists slowly and be ruthlessly honest. Ask yourself if any of these symptoms exist in your life.

Symptoms of a Lack of Intimacy

- Difficulty beginning new relationships
- Passivity and detachment from others
- Seeing yourself as a victim
- Denying or hiding your feelings
- Using addictions and other behaviors to numb feelings
- Reluctance to ask for help
- Maintaining an unrealistic workload
- Privacy
- Minimizing the feelings of others
- Struggling with honesty in relationships
- Avoiding conflict
- Using anger to control others
- Avoiding direct communications
- Refusing to take risks

- Taking yourself too seriously
- No hobbies (unless they are compulsive, competitive, or income producing).[3]

Poor Substitutions

- Excessive TV watching, Internet use, or other isolating activities (even reading or study, when used as an escape)
- Compulsive hobbies
- Overeating
- Oversleeping
- Angry outbursts
- Chronic bitterness
- Workaholism
- Emotional or physical infidelity
- Pornography
- Drug or alcohol use[4]

Intimacy Regained

The road to intimacy leads down the path of honesty. Honesty inevitably leads to disclosure and confession.

During Jesus' time on earth, the apostle John was one of His closest friends. John is noted for his affection for Jesus (John 13:23). John's three letters reveal the supreme value he placed on love and relationships (see 1 John 2:3–15; 3:1–18, 23; 4:7–12, 16–21; 5:1–3; 2 John 1–6; 3 John 1–9). John addresses the requirement of confession and honesty, which lead to both vertical and horizontal intimacy.

John uses the metaphor of light to mark a pure, authentic, clear, bright relationship. God dwells in such a state with Himself. If we want to experience an unclouded relationship with God *and* with others, we must choose to walk in the light.

> *This is the message we have heard from him and declare to you: God is light; in him there is no darkness at all. If we claim to have fellowship with him and yet walk in the darkness, we lie and do not live out the truth. But if we walk in the light, as he is in the light, we have fellowship with one another, and the blood of Jesus, his Son, purifies us from all sin.*
>
> 1 JOHN 1:5–7

John says that the issue of sin must be faced courageously if we're to enjoy fellowship with God and with others. Unresolved sin darkens our relationships. Choosing to sin is like walking into the shadows. Therefore, we must confess sin, fear, shame, and guilt. Then God will forgive us, and we can walk in the light with Him and really experience a shared and close relationship with others.

> *If we claim to be without sin, we deceive ourselves and the truth is not in us. If we confess our sins, he is faithful and just and will forgive us our*

sins and purify us from all unrighteousness. If we claim we have not sinned, we make him out to be a liar and his word is not in us.

1 JOHN 1:8–10

The key is our willingness to confess our sins. The term *confess* literally means "to say the same thing; to assent, agree with, concede; declare; acknowledge guilt." As we see our sin as God sees it, personally acknowledging it, we step out of the shadows into the sunshine. Honesty is the path to intimacy.

Unconquered until Uncovered

Honesty is the path to intimacy. Note what Proverbs says:

Whoever conceals their sins does not prosper, but the one who confesses and renounces them finds mercy.

PROVERBS 28:13

Concealing our sins, hiding, and refusing to confess shuts us off from the grace of God. Confessing and renouncing our sin positions us to receive mercy.

In other words, sin is unconquered until it is uncovered.

Men who struggle with a healthy closeness to God and with other men often have intimacy issues with women as well. They also find themselves struggling with strongholds they just cannot shake on their own. These usually include anger, lust, pornography, alcohol or drug abuse, gambling, or work addiction. Often it stems from hurt and distance in their relationship with their earthly father.

Over and over again, I have seen men who have struggled with the same sins for years find grace and victory when they confess the sins to God in the company of others. Sin begins to be conquered when sin is uncovered. If men will engage in an ongoing, authentic relationship that includes accountability with a few other men, they can experience true and lasting victory.

There Is No Healing in Hiding

History tells us that Jesus' half brother James served as one of the leaders of the large church of Jerusalem. Eventually many of his flock were scattered because of fierce persecution. James wrote them a letter in which he also pointed to honesty as the pathway to intimacy. I especially like Eugene Peterson's rendering of James's instructions.

> *Make this your common practice: Confess your sins to each other and pray for each other so that you can live together whole and healed.*
> JAMES 5:16 MSG

Note that healing is the result of confession to one another.

Many of us were taught to confess our sins only to God, but that is not what James says. He says confess "to each other."

Let me also point out that the verb tense of the term *confess* speaks to continual action. The act of honestly confessing to each other was not to be merely a one-time act, but rather an ongoing, common practice.

Note also that once sin is confessed, the confessor is not to be left high and dry. He or she is to be prayed for, and those prayers are also to be an ongoing, regular, and common practice.

Finally, notice that the result of authentic, honest confession and prayer is healing. Peterson places it in context when he writes, "So that you can live together whole and healed." The word *heal* means "to cure, make whole, restore; to bring about salvation." James is telling us that open, ongoing confession of sin to others who will respond with prayer opens the door to an outpouring of God's grace. Physical healing, emotional wholeness, relational restoration, and deliverance from besetting sins are all possible.

Kevin Miller writes, "Confession to another Christian is not only commanded in the Bible (James 5:16), it's the door to healing and holiness."[5] Richard Foster says that this type of confession is more than psychologically therapeutic. "It involves an objective change in our relationship with God and a subjective change in us. It is a means of healing and transforming the inner spirit."[6]

I have seen the power of such confession not only in my life but in the lives of many others. The chains of lifelong sins have been broken. Deep wounds have been healed. Relationships with God have been restored.

But there is even more than the vertical and internal blessings that flow when true confession occurs. Honesty leads to intimacy with others.

Come Out of Hiding

We have discussed confessing sins as the path to intimacy, but the life of honesty goes beyond exposure of sin to *disclosure* of ourselves. In order to experience close and full relationships with God and others, we must live open, authentic lives. We must regularly and ruthlessly expose and admit our sins *and* disclose our scars, secrets, and struggles.

We all need the healing that comes from disclosing our scars.

As a teenager, I had a battle with lust and pornography. At various points, I was so discouraged that I wanted to give up on my Christian life. But one day, I gathered the courage to share with a few trusted friends that I had been exposed to pornography as a seven-year-old boy. I was hoping that they would not reject me or disrespect me. They didn't. They prayed for me and shared their own scars. Deep healing and closeness resulted.

We all need a few trusted friends with whom we can disclose our secrets.

I was talking with a close friend recently. We have known each other several years and have become close through honesty and openness. He told me that I am one of very few people on earth that he trusts completely. Then I asked him a very specific question about his past. He gulped and replied, "I have never told anyone this before, but. . ." and he proceeded to tell me his deepest, darkest secret.

We all need the relief that comes from sharing our struggles.

One night at our small group Bible study, I was paired up to pray with my neighbor. He's a great guy and seemed to have it all together, without a care in the world. This was the third or fourth time he and I had been paired up, and usually his prayer requests centered on his children—never anything about himself. But this time I guess he was feeling a level of trust with me. He dropped his head, rubbed his forehead, and sighed deeply. "I still can't find a job," he said, "and it's killing me." Just the simple act of telling me his struggle seemed to lighten his load immensely and gave us the beginnings of a deeper friendship.

What Now?

Jesus modeled a life of utter transparency and disclosure with a few trusted friends. Obviously He had no sins to confess. But He did allow his followers and friends to see Him up close. He allowed His friends to see Him in unguarded moments of joy, sadness, anger, fatigue, and soul anguish. And they loved him for it.

I have learned the joy of living an open life. The pressure to protect, the fatigue of trying to cover up, is gone. As a result of my willingness to be appropriately open with others, others have been much more open with me. As a result, my relationships are better than ever. Honesty is the forgotten key to intimacy and a secret to better relationships.

Notes

1. Ortberg, *Everybody's Normal*, 72–73.
2. Michael Todd Wilson and Brad Hoffmann, *Preventing Ministry Failure* (Downers Grove, IL: InterVarsity, 2007), 38.
3. Adapted from Wilson and Hoffmann, *Preventing Ministry Failure*, 39.
4. Ibid., 40.
5. Kevin Miller, "Church Discipline for Repetitive Sin," *LeadershipJournal. net* (May 22, 2009): http://www.christianitytoday.com/le/communitylife /discipleship/churchdisciplinerepetitivesin.html?start=1.
6. Richard Foster, *Celebration of Discipline* (San Francisco: HarperSanFrancisco, 1998), 144.

8

Encourage

"Mr. Encouragement"

Imagine being such a consummate and consistent encourager that others recognize it and call you "Mr. Encouragement." That was the name given to a first-century Christian named "Joseph, a Levite from Cyprus, whom the apostles called Barnabas (which means 'son of encouragement')" (Acts 4:36). And he lived up to it.

The first time we see Barnabas mentioned in scripture is early in the history of the church. He encourages the entire church of Jerusalem in a tangible, practical way through a timely act of radical generosity (Acts 4:37).

The second time Barnabas appears in Acts, he extends himself to help an unknown, zealous young preacher named Saul. The man later called Paul had been a fierce persecutor of the church but was miraculously converted to Christianity—and now wanted to join the disciples in Jerusalem. But because of Saul's reputation, the apostles were skeptical of his motives for wanting to see them. Barnabas believed in Saul when no one else did. He personally took Saul to meet the apostles and strongly endorsed him (Acts 9:26–27).

Next Barnabas was called to help establish the new church in Antioch. The ministry was flourishing and he needed help. So he went out of his way to get Saul to aid him with the teaching (Acts 11:22–26). He gave Saul an opportunity he would not otherwise have had.

The fourth time Barnabas is mentioned, he and Saul are listed among the leaders of the church in Antioch. Interestingly, he is listed first, Saul last. The next thing we know, they are called out as church-planting missionaries. By the end of the chapter, Saul is being called Paul and is listed first, indicating leadership (Acts 13:42). Barnabas was willing to stand aside and give Paul a chance to lead.

Barnabas's belief in Saul paid off.

Humanly speaking, the great apostle Paul would not have gotten far in his role as a missionary, church planter, author, and leading light of Christianity if not for Barnabas. Never underestimate the power of timely encouragement!

Sometime later, as the two men were preparing for another missionary journey, Barnabas did it again. Previously, he and Paul had taken a young man named John Mark with them on their missionary journey. But for some reason Mark had bailed out, leaving early. In Paul's zealous mind, Mark had blown it beyond repair. So this time, as they got ready to go, Paul did not want to take Mark along (Acts 15:36–38).

But Barnabas saw things differently. He looked at Mark through the eyes of an encourager. So he gave Mark a second chance, taking him along though that meant Barnabas and Paul went separate ways (Acts 15:39).

Barnabas's belief in Mark paid off.

Instead of becoming a castoff, Mark eventually regained Paul's favor (Colossians 4:10; 2 Timothy 4:11; Philemon 24). Mark also accompanied Peter at one time (1 Peter 5:13). Ultimately, Mark wrote the Gospel of Mark. Never underestimate the power of timely encouragement!

The word *encouragement* speaks of coming alongside others and giving them courage. Life can be a fearful thing. Everyone needs someone drawing alongside, saying, "You can do it. Don't quit." Everyone needs someone who believes in them. Everyone needs encouragement.

Secret #8
Encourage others.

For the Greeks, the heart was the center of a person's inner life, the source of all forces and functions of the inner being. To be *discouraged* was to "lose heart; to have the very core of your being cut out." *Encouragement,* therefore, means to "put the heart back" or "put the courage back" into someone.

Encouragement is not something we can offer others from a safe distance. The word rendered as *encourage* most often in the New Testament is a compound word combining the word for "call out or invite" and the word for "alongside of." It speaks of helping restore a failing heart, rekindle a burnt-out heart; and heal a broken heart.

The word *encourage* is used 109 times in the Bible and has various shades of meaning. A full-blown definition of the biblical notion of encouragement would go something like this:

Encouragement: to come alongside someone in order to comfort, console, cheer up, cheer on, counsel, call out, challenge, exhort, entreat, strengthen, teach, instruct, admonish, warn, urge, appeal, beg, or beseech.

Encouraging others is a command to be obeyed, a ministry to be practiced, and a lifestyle to be lived. It is essential for building relationships.

The Many-Sided, Mutual Ministry of Encouragement

If any group of people needed encouragement, the first-century Jewish Christians did. Persecution was fierce. Their property was plundered. Many were being mistreated, some thrown in prison (Hebrews 10:32–34; 13:3). Hated by their fellow Jews and oppressed by pagans, they lived as virtual fugitives.

An encourager wrote them a letter that is now contained in the Bible—the book of Hebrews. (Some scholars believe the author was none other than. . .Barnabas). Whoever wrote the letter was a master encourager. Twelve times he encourages the Hebrew Christians to band together and challenge each other to higher living, even despite their suffering (see Hebrews 4:1, 11–16; 6:1; 10:22–24; 12:1, 28; 13:13–15).

To illustrate the importance of a mutual ministry of encouragement, I selected several translations of the same passage—Hebrews 10:24–25. As you read the different versions, note the variety of ways we are to encourage one other. Note also that this many-sided, mutual ministry of encouragement is to be an ongoing, continual lifestyle.

*Let's see how inventive we can be in **encouraging** love and helping out, not avoiding worshiping together as some do but **spurring each other on**, especially as we see the big Day approaching.*
HEBREWS 10:24–25 MSG

120

*And let us consider and give attentive, continuous care to watching over one another, studying how we may **stir up (stimulate and incite)** to love and helpful deeds and noble activities, Not forsaking or neglecting to assemble together [as believers], as is the habit of some people, but **admonishing (warning, urging, and encouraging) one another**, and all the more faithfully as you see the day approaching.*
HEBREWS 10:24–25 AMP

*Let us think of ways to **motivate one another** to acts of love and good works. And let us not neglect our meeting together, as some people do, but **encourage one another**, especially now that the day of his return is drawing near.*
HEBREWS 10:24–25 NLT

*We should **keep on encouraging** each other to be thoughtful and to do helpful things. Some people have gotten out of the habit of meeting for worship, but we must not do that. We should **keep on encouraging** each other, especially since you know that the day of the Lord's coming is getting closer.*
HEBREWS 10:24–25 CEV

Encourage One Another

Barnabas passed on his passion for encouragement to the apostle Paul, his top student. Paul then commanded his followers to practice the art of encouragement.

> *Finally, brothers and sisters, rejoice! Strive for full restoration,*
> ***encourage one another***, *be of one mind, live in peace.*
> *And the God of love and peace will be with you.*
> 2 CORINTHIANS 13:11

> *Therefore* ***encourage one another*** *and build*
> *each other up, just as in fact you are doing.*
> 1 THESSALONIANS 5:11

> *And we urge you, brothers and sisters, warn those*
> *who are idle and disruptive,* ***encourage*** *the disheartened,*
> *help the weak, be patient with everyone.*
> 1 THESSALONIANS 5:14

Paul did not merely instruct others to be people of encouragement, he lived it. For example, when Paul and Barnabas visited the Macedonian city of Lystra to plant a church, opposition there was so severe that a mob stoned Paul to the point of death. Paul knew this persecution would have scared the fledgling church at Lystra, so he used his own willingness to suffer for Christ to challenge, strengthen, and encourage the new converts.

> *After proclaiming the Message in Derbe and establishing a strong core of disciples, they retraced their steps to Lystra, then Iconium, and then Antioch, **putting muscle and sinew in the lives of the disciples, urging them to stick with what they had begun to believe and not quit**, making it clear to them that it wouldn't be easy: "Anyone signing up for the kingdom of God has to go through plenty of hard times."*
> ACTS 14:21–22 MSG

Later Paul and his missionary partner Silas visited the city of Philippi in order to start a church. This time they ended up in prison for their faith. As you may recall, God sent a small earthquake that opened the prison doors and led both to the conversion of the jailer and to Paul and Silas's release. Note what happened next.

> *So [Paul and Silas] left the prison and went to Lydia's house; and when they had seen the brethren, they **warned and urged and consoled and encouraged** them and departed.*
> ACTS 16:40 AMP

Later, after Paul started a church in Ephesus, a riot erupted over his ministry. Again the church would have been spooked by the persecution Paul faced. Note what he did next.

*After the uproar had ceased, Paul sent for the disciples and **warned
and consoled and urged and encouraged** them; then he embraced them
and told them farewell and set forth on his journey to Macedonia.*

ACTS 20:1 AMP

God may have allowed you to experience some dark days and
tough times. How might you use what you have experienced to
challenge others to greater faith, higher hope, and deeper love?

"Nobody Had Ever Said I Was Good at Anything"

Author Donald Miller attributes his eventual success as a writer
to the encouragement he received in middle school from David
Gentiles, his church's youth pastor. At the time, Miller was a
mixed up young man who had both shoplifted and broken into
people's homes. Having grown up without a father, he mistrusted
and rebelled against men in authority.

But all that changed when David Gentiles came along. A
Louisiana Cajun who stood only five foot five, Gentiles had an
impact well beyond his physical stature. According to Miller,
Gentiles "taught me more about Jesus than anybody I knew. . . .
Being friends with David was an uneven deal. You could not love
him like he loved you."[1]

Gentiles had a knack for seeing potential in people and
encouraging them to reach it. He convinced Miller to start writing

and peppered him with positive feedback. Miller later said, "Nobody [had ever] said I was good at anything. This was the first time tasting that. It was like water for thirst."[2]

Who Knows What Could Have Been?

Former school teacher Florence Littauer has become a legendary motivational speaker and best-selling author of more than twenty books.

Unfortunately, her father's dream of becoming a writer himself never came to fruition.

Littauer tells of how she discovered her father's secret ambition when she came home for Christmas vacation during her senior year of college. When she and her father were alone, he pulled her aside into the little family den, reached behind the old upright piano, and pulled out a battered cigar box. Opening it, he showed her a pile of newspaper articles.

"These are articles I have written and some letters to the editor that have been published," he said.

Florence was shocked. "Why didn't you tell me you could write?" she asked.

"Because I didn't want your mother to know," he said. "She's always told me that since I didn't have much education I shouldn't try to write. I wanted to run for some political office also, but she told me I shouldn't try."

"I figured I could write without her knowing it," he continued. "When each item would be printed, I'd cut it out and hide it in this box."

The next day Florence's parents got on a bus to take a brief, yet much needed, vacation from their family store. That night she looked out the window and saw her mother get off the bus—alone.

"Where's Dad?" Florence asked.

"Your father's dead."

He had died at the Boston bus station earlier in the day.

Years later, Florence looked back.

"Father left me no money, but he left me the box. He had little education and no degrees, but he gave me and my brothers a love for the English language, a thirst for politics, and an ability to write. Who knows what Father could have done with just a little encouragement?"[3]

Believe in Others

Encouragement is one of the most powerful relationship builders we can practice. Everyone loves an encourager

I was a very shy high school student. Yet my youth pastor, Lee Simmons, kept encouraging and pushing me to get out of my comfort zone and minister. He "made" me share a testimony before the youth group, he "begged" me to be in the youth choir, he "twisted my arm" to give the devotional at a large youth gathering.

He believed in me when no one else did. Humanly speaking, I would not be in ministry today without Lee's encouragement.

When I was a college student, I sensed God calling me to plant a church. Dr. Elmer Towns was one of the few people who expressed belief in my ability to plant a successful church. That was a giant encouragement I desperately needed. Since then I have trained hundreds of church planters. I probably would not have become a church planter had it not been for Dr. Towns's encouragement. Everyone needs someone to believe in them.

What Now?

Let me encourage you to. . .become a master encourager. It does not require talent or skill, just a positive attitude and a willing heart. I believe you can do it. Allow me to give you a few suggestions to get you started:

- Ask God to guide you into the best way to encourage each person in your life.
- Encourage others by believing in them.
- Set people up for success, not failure.
- Tell people when they are doing a good job.
- Point out everything others do right.
- Encourage others by helping them with some part of the process.
- Speak highly of other people in front of others.

127

Notes

1. Information for this story adapted from John Blake, "Born-again Rebel Don Miller Reveals 'Best Sermon I Ever Heard,'" CNN.com, July 19, 2010, 3-4; http://articles.cnn.com/2010-07-19/living/Miller.jazz_1_donald-miller-evangelicals-miller-appeals?_s=PM:LIVING.

2. Ibid., 4.

3. Adapted from Florence Littauer, *Silver Boxes: The Gift of Encouragement* (Dallas: Word, 1989), 124–128.

9

Pray

Pray for each other so that you may be healed.
The prayer of a righteous person is powerful and effective.
JAMES 5:16

Old Camel Knees

Doc. Dubya. Fats. MJ. Big Boy. A-Rod. J-Lo. The Red Baron. Baby-kins. Stonewall. Romeo. Ace. Old Faithful. Maverick. Honey Bunch. Champ. Caped Crusader. Pookie Bear. Old Camel Knees.

Old Camel Knees? I bet that's a nickname you haven't heard recently. But it can unlock the door to better relationships. Track with me as I explain.

Jesus was the virgin-born Son of God. After Jesus was born, Joseph and Mary had other children, at least four boys and several girls (Matthew 13:55–56; Mark 6:3). James was the eldest of these, making him a half-brother of Jesus (Galatians 1:18–20). Like his siblings, James was unwilling to believe that Jesus was God

(John 7:3–5) until after Jesus rose from the dead (1 Corinthians 15:3–7). After James's conversion, he rose quickly to a place of top leadership in the church at Jerusalem (Acts 15:13–21; 21:17–18; Galatians 2:9–12).

Viewing prayer as a primary means of ministering, James devoted himself to going to the temple, kneeling on the stone floor, and praying for his flock. Tradition holds that he spent so much time on his knees that thick calluses built up, like those on the knees of a camel. So James was called "Old Camel Knees."

When intense persecution hit Jerusalem, many in the church were scattered across the Near East. Hated by both the Jews and the pagans, they faced severe trials, hostility, and persecution.

James prayed for them.

Also James wrote them a letter to encourage them. That letter is found in the Bible and is named after its author. At the end of the letter, James drops in a word of advice based on his experience.

> *Pray for each other so that you may be healed.*
> *The prayer of a righteous person is powerful and effective.*
> JAMES 5:16

James knew that one of the best ways for his scattered flock to remain strong and close was by praying with and for each other. Prayer is an often overlooked secret to better relationships.

Secret #9
Pray for one another.

Pray for Each Other

Though the apostle Paul was driven by a sense of calling unlike few men in history, he was a wisely relational man. He got his start under the tutelage of Barnabas (Acts 9:27), who gave him ministry experience in Antioch (Acts 11:19–30) and took him along on a church-planting journey (Acts 13:2–4). Paul later "paid it forward" by investing deeply in the lives of Luke, Titus, Silas, and Timothy, as they ministered alongside him.

The role of *friend* was one Paul took very seriously as he taught, modeled, encouraged, and especially prayed for others. Fortunately for us, he recorded many of the prayers he offered on behalf of his friends. From those prayers we learn a great deal about how we can pray for our friends.

In one sitting, I read the content of each of Paul's prayers, in four translations. Wow! Reading them all at once shook me, convicted me, challenged me, and powerfully encouraged me to pray for others. (These prayers are found in Romans 1:8–10; 15: 5–6, 13; Ephesians 1:15–19; 3:14–19; Philippians 1:9–11; Colossians 1:9–12; 1 Thessalonians 1:2–3; 3:11–13; 2 Thessalonians 1:11–12;

Philemon 4–6). Looking at all these prayers together helps us learn how to pray for others.

1. Pray consistently

The first thing that jumps out as we study Paul's prayers is his repeated mention of how consistently and constantly he prayed for others. Obviously, Paul viewed regular, consistent, frequent, fervent, constant prayer as a primary responsibility toward his spiritual children. Note the words italicized below:

- Romans 1:9 (NKJV): "*Without ceasing* I make mention of you *always* in my prayers."
- Ephesians 1:16: "*I have not stopped* giving thanks for you, remembering you in my prayers."
- Colossians 1:3 (NKJV): "We give thanks. . .*praying always* for you."
- 1 Thessalonians 1:2 (ESV): "We give thanks to God *always* for all of you, *constantly mentioning you* in our prayers."
- 1 Thessalonians 3:10 (NLT): "*Night and day we pray earnestly for you.*"
- 2 Thessalonians 1:11: "We *constantly* pray for you."
- 2 Timothy 1:3 (NKJV): "*Without ceasing* I remember you in my prayers night and day."
- Philemon 4 (ESV): "I thank my God *always* when I remember you in my prayers."

Look back through those verses and observe the drumbeat repetition describing the consistency of Paul's prayers for his spiritual children: "without ceasing," "have not stopped," "praying always," "always," "night and day," "constantly." You get the idea that he never skipped a day, let alone missed an opportunity, to pray for his friends. Every time they came to mind, he offered a prayer on their behalf.

Maybe you're like I am. I will pray a lot when there is an emergency or crisis, but I tend to slack off when the pressure's off. I need to learn to pray more consistently, even when there is no crisis. If I did, maybe there would be fewer crises.

My guess is that most of us would have to say that the frequency of our prayers for those we love is too little—and often, too late. I encourage you to establish a set time, at least once a day, when you pray for your loved ones.

2. Pray gratefully

Paul was not only consistent in his prayers, he was also constant in his gratitude. Again and again he mentions how thankful he is for his spiritual children and the work God has already done and is doing in them. Read the following verses and note Paul's heartbeat of gratitude:

- Romans 1:8: "First, I *thank* my God through Jesus Christ for all of you."

- 1 Corinthians 1:4: "I always *thank* my God for you because of his grace given you in Christ Jesus."
- Ephesians 1:15–16: "Ever since I heard about your faith in the Lord Jesus and your love for all God's people, I have not stopped *giving thanks* for you."
- Philippians 1:3: "I *thank* my God every time I remember you."
- Colossians 1:3: "We always *thank* God, the Father of our Lord Jesus Christ, when we pray for you."
- 1 Thessalonians 1:2: "We always *thank* God for all of you and continually mention you in our prayers."
- 1 Thessalonians 2:13: "We also *thank* God continually."
- 1 Thessalonians 3:9: "How can we *thank* God enough for you?"
- 2 Thessalonians 1:3: "We ought always to *thank* God for you."
- 2 Timothy 1:3: "I *thank* God, whom I serve. . .as night and day I constantly remember you in my prayers."
- Philemon 4: "I always *thank* my God as I remember you in my prayers."

Do you thank God for your loved ones every day? Or are you like I am, often taking for granted that God has given them to you as a gift, that He is already working in their lives? We should learn from Paul to spend time each day thanking God for others.

Maintaining strong relationships can be one of the most discouraging tasks we ever face. Some go through stretches when it is, at best, three steps forward, two steps back.

Paul built and maintained effective relationships with people who could have worn him out and driven him crazy. But they didn't make him bitter, cynical, or discouraged. Why? *He always thanked God for them.* What I find challenging is that Paul was not only thankful for the faith of the Romans and the influential Thessalonians, but he was also grateful for the carnal Corinthians. His Corinthian children were always struggling to follow his leadership. They continually fought with each other. They got off track easily, quickly, and often.

We should note not only *that* Paul was grateful, but also *what* he was grateful for. He didn't thank God for the people's good health or easy lives. Instead he was grateful to God for what He had done in their lives, what He was doing in their lives, and what He would do in their lives. Paul's basis of gratitude was *spiritual*, not physical or material. I am not saying we shouldn't thank God for the physical, material, educational, and vocational blessings He gives our loved ones. But the primary content of our gratitude should be focused on the spiritual work He has, is, and has yet to do in their lives.

3. Pray expectantly

Paul was not only consistent in his prayers and constant in his gratitude, he was also confident in his expectation. He prayed believing that God was not finished yet. God still had more and better ahead. Let's look at several examples:

May the God of hope fill you with all joy and peace as you trust in him,
so that you may overflow with hope by the power of the Holy Spirit.
I myself am convinced, my brothers and sisters, that you yourselves are full of
goodness, filled with knowledge and competent to instruct one another.

ROMANS 15:13–14

Notice that Paul bases his prayers on the confidence he has in the people for whom he prays. Because God is in them, they have goodness, knowledge, and ability.

I always thank my God for you because of his grace given you in Christ
Jesus. For in him you have been enriched in every way—with all kinds of
speech and with all knowledge—God thus confirming our testimony about
Christ among you. Therefore you do not lack any spiritual gift as you eagerly
wait for our Lord Jesus Christ to be revealed. He will also keep you firm to the
end, so that you will be blameless on the day of our Lord Jesus Christ. God is
faithful, who has called you into fellowship with his Son, Jesus Christ our Lord.

1 CORINTHIANS 1:4–9

Note that this is what he prays for the Corinthians, his most troublesome group of spiritual children. Yet he is confident that one day even they will end up blameless, because *God is faithful.* We can pray for our friends with great expectation and great confidence because we are praying to a great and faithful God.

I thank my God upon every remembrance of you, always in every prayer of mine making request for you all with joy, for your fellowship in the gospel from the first day until now, being confident of this very thing, that He who has begun a good work in you will complete it until the day of Jesus Christ.

PHILIPPIANS 1:3–6 NKJV

Note carefully verse 6. Paul says that he prayed from a foundation of confidence that the same God who had begun a good work in these people would complete it. I like how Eugene Peterson renders this verse in The Message: "There has never been the slightest doubt in my mind that the God who started this great work in you would keep at it and bring it to a flourishing finish on the very day Christ Jesus appears." There will be times when others disappoint us. We must be like Paul and remember that our faith is not so much in them as it is in God, who is at work in them. As long as they are breathing, God is not finished working.

Now to him who is able to do immeasurably more than all we ask or imagine, according to the power that is at work within us, to him be glory in the church and in Christ Jesus throughout all generations, for ever and ever! Amen.

EPHESIANS 3:20–21

Read these verses again, slowly. What an encouraging promise! We pour our hearts out to God on behalf of our loved ones, and it not only makes us feel better, it accomplishes something. God is able! He can do far more than we could ever imagine or guess or request in our wildest dreams. He is powerful. His power works in us and in our loved ones, so that it ultimately adds up to His glory.

Too often the aim of our prayers is much too low. Paul prayed expecting that others wouldn't just barely make God's team and ride the bench but that they would hit spiritual home runs and end up in the hall of faith. God is able and willing to work. He can do more than we can ask or imagine.

4. Pray spiritually
Paul was not only consistent in his prayers, constant in his gratitude, and confident in his expectation, he was also consumed with his flock's spiritual progress. He prayed that they would know God and all God had available for them (Ephesians 1:17–19); that they would have inner strength and live open to Christ, experiencing the full dimensions of His love (Ephesians 3:14–20); and that they'd learn to live wisely and bear spiritual fruit (Philippians 1:9–11). Paul also prayed that they'd be in step with God's will and live well as they worked for Him with glorious and joyful endurance (Colossians 1:9–12); that they'd overflow with love, strength, and purity (1 Thessalonians 3:11–13); and that God would make them holy and whole inside and out (1 Thessalonians 5:23–24). Paul prayed that they'd be fit for what God had called them to be; that God would energize their efforts (2 Thessalonians 1:11–12); that

they'd experience spiritual encouragement and empowerment in their words and works (2 Thessalonians 2:16–17); and that as they shared their faith they would understand just how amazing it was (Philemon 6).

Unlike most of our prayers, which tend to be based on physical needs, vocational challenges, and financial circumstances, Paul's prayers are consumed with the spiritual state of his loved ones. I'm sure he mentioned other areas of need on occasion, but what comprised the vast majority of his requests was their spiritual condition.

Beyond that he prayed they would not remain at their current levels of spiritual maturity. Repeatedly his prayers are entwined with requests for their ongoing spiritual development and progress. For example, Paul asks that they would "[grow] in the knowledge of God" (Colossians 1:10) and "increase and abound in love to one another and to all" (1 Thessalonians 3:12 NKJV). He also tells them he prays that their "faith grows exceedingly, and the love of every one of you all abounds toward each other" (2 Thessalonians 1:3 NKJV).

As I read Paul's prayers, I come away with the strong sense that I need to make some changes. The content of my prayers is too often temporal, external, and superficial. We can learn from Paul to focus our prayers on that which is most important—the spiritual development of our loved ones.

Pray with Others

To fully capitalize on the power of relationships through prayer, we need to pray not only *for* each other but also *with* each other.

Evelyn Christenson wrote several bestselling books about prayer, including *What Happens When Women Pray*. She views praying with others as a powerful, yet often untapped, secret. She writes, "[People praying together] is the secret that has undergirded me with physical strength when there was none in my body. It has called down God's powerful movement in ministry. And, amazingly, this secret has resulted in an exchange of my finite limitations for so much of God's promised infinite power. . . . I have experienced awesome results from my solitary prayers; but I have also found the added comfort, support and love of those who have faithfully and persistently prayed with me."[1]

Jesus prayed for His followers (John 17), but He also encouraged them—and us—to pray together. He said that praying together gets results.

> *"Again, truly I tell you that if two of you on earth agree about anything they ask for, it will be done for them by my Father in heaven."*
> MATTHEW 18:19

Here's how Eugene Peterson paraphrases this statement in The Message: "When two of you get together on anything at all on earth and make a prayer of it, my Father in heaven goes into action." Imagine that! By praying together, we invite God's active involvement.

Jesus also promised that praying together draws us closer to God and to each other.

> *"For where two or three gather in my name,*
> *there am I with them."*
> MATTHEW 18:20

I had a roommate during my first year of college who was a really great Christian guy. (He is a US Army chaplain today.) But our personalities were so different that we struggled to get along. After several weeks of frustration, we mutually decided that we needed help. . .from God. So we made a covenant to pray together every night at eleven o'clock. It was a small thing, but it made a huge difference. It drew us closer to God and to each other.

Praying together not only works with friends and roommates, it especially works with married couples. Over the past twenty years, dozens of surveys have revealed the positive benefits of prayer on marital happiness. For example, one very recent survey states that couples who pray together "hold hands more often. They make love more often. They respect each other more, compliment more, and bicker less."[2]

According to Les and Leslie Parrott, "Prayer is a more

powerful predictor of marital happiness than frequency of sexual intimacy."[3] Another study showed that couples who frequently prayed together were twice as likely as those who prayed less often to describe their marriages as highly romantic. They also reported higher sexual satisfaction. Most tellingly, with a national divorce rate of one out of every two marriages, of those couples who were married in a church, attended regularly, and *prayed together* as a couple, the divorce rate was only 1 out of 1105![4]

What Now?

Apply what you have read. Take the next few minutes and pray for the close people in your life. Even better, pray *with* them.

Notes

1. Evelyn Christenson, from the Foreword to Elmer L. Towns, *Prayer Partners* (Ventura, CA: Regal, 2002).

2. Quoted in *The Fort Worth Star-Telegram*, "Praying Together Means More Than Staying Together, Authors Say," February 14, 2008.

3. Les and Leslie Parrott, *Saving Your Marriage Before It Starts* (Grand Rapids: Zondervan, 2006), 150–151.

4. This statistic is quoted in *Building a Foundation for the Family*, an audio series by John C. Maxwell, (Injoy, 1992).

10

Make Peace

"Be at peace with each other."
MARK 9:50

Live in harmony with one another.
ROMANS 12:16

"Blessed are the peacemakers, for they will be called children of God."
MATTHEW 5:9

Brian and Lindsey were both committed Christians and had been married for several years. Everyone considered Brian and Lindsey to be very nice people. They were both generous with their time and money. Yet neither one handled conflict well.

In the wake of the inevitable conflicts a new couple faces, their marriage was starting to unravel. Though they sincerely loved God and each other, it was as if they were always at war. When conflict hit, Lindsey usually yelled and attacked Brian. Brian often said nothing, but he harbored resentment deep inside. After a big fight, he might go days without speaking to Lindsey.

Growing up, neither Brian nor Lindsey had learned how to resolve conflict wisely. Brian's family never fought about anything. Conflict was avoided at all costs, yet grudges were carried for years and resentments ran deep. Several members of his family were no longer speaking with one another.

Lindsey's family, on the other hand, argued all the time, with angry shouting and ugly threats. In spite of the noise, the issues were never decided and the hurts never healed. They fought over the same unresolved issues again and again.

After one particularly ugly fight with Lindsey, Brian had had enough. He packed a suitcase and moved out of the house that night. Though he did not believe that divorce was right, he got up the next morning and went to a lawyer to draw up papers. He couldn't take it anymore. Brian and Lindsey's failure to understand and practice the essentials of peacemaking was killing their marriage.

Secret #10
Choose to make peace.

The Truth about Conflict

1. Conflict is inevitable

If two people are around each other for very long, conflict will result. We are all different. We have unique personalities, tastes, habits, preferences, experiences, passions, and ways of looking at and navigating life. These distinctions create differences. Beyond that, most of us live at a very fast pace, which naturally creates friction. Plus, we each have a fallen nature and live in a fallen world. That world throws stressful situations and painful circumstances at us. We're not always at our best all the time. So conflicts arise. Someone feels misunderstood, wronged, denied, or unappreciated.

When relationships start, they are usually built on three factors: things we have in common; things about us that are different, but complementary; and things that are different and *not* complementary. The third factor is what causes friction.

No matter how deeply a man and woman love each other, no matter how long two friends have known each other, no matter how mature two Christians are in spiritual matters, they will eventually have conflict in that third area. It is unrealistic to expect otherwise.

2. Conflict that goes unresolved devastates relationships

Conflict in and of itself is not a problem. It is neutral—neither bad nor good. The goodness or badness of conflict depends on how we respond to it. If we fail to make peace effectively, our relationships will suffer.

Unresolved conflict is the ugly elephant-in-the-room or lethal cancer in too many failed relationships. Unresolved conflict will eventually erode the joy, rob the peace, and shred the commitments from our relationships.

3. Conflict is an assignment, not an accident

Ken Sande, founder of Peacemaker Ministries, joined with a group of pastors, lawyers, and business people who wanted to encourage and assist Christians in responding to conflict biblically. As part of the peacemaker's pledge he states that "conflict is an assignment, not an accident."[1]

Our sovereign God might not create conflicts, but He often allows them to arise in our relationships for our good and His ultimate glory. Therefore we need to realize that conflict is always an opportunity.

Conflict can either be very destructive or very beneficial, depending on how it is handled. Every conflict we experience has great potential. When handled well, conflict can make us better, give us stronger relationships, and glorify God.

Jesus applauded peacemakers. In His teachings on true happiness, He said that peacemaking is an opportunity for us to discover ourselves and our place in God's family, experience deeper personal satisfaction, and reflect the image of God.

> *"Blessed are the peacemakers, for they will be called children of God."*
> MATTHEW 5:9

Jesus also prayed for peacemakers. In the agonizing prayer He offered to His Father just hours before dying on the cross, Jesus prayed that His followers would become peacemakers and thereby experience true unity.

> *"My prayer is not for them alone. I pray also for those who will believe in me through their message, that all of them may be one, Father, just as you are in me and I am in you. May they also be in us so that the world may believe that you have sent me."*
> JOHN 17:20–21

Conflict is a necessary part of close relationships. It is always an opportunity to grow and to glorify God. Learn to view conflict as an assignment, not an accident.

4. Conflict does not resolve itself
The path of least resistance is not the solution to relational conflicts. When faced with conflict, some people try to avoid it entirely. But pretending that conflict doesn't exist does not solve the situation and will ultimately make matters worse.

Others acknowledge that conflict exists but refuse to take action. This also accelerates and compounds problems (Genesis 16:1–6; 1 Samuel 2:22–25).

Still others try to escape conflict by ending the relationship, quitting the job, filing for divorce, or changing churches (Genesis 16:6–8). Their world gets smaller and smaller as they bail out of every relationship when it starts getting difficult.

5. Conflict cannot be ignored
The path of least resistance is not the solution to relational conflicts. Conflict does not resolve itself. Conflict must be courageously addressed. Jesus made it clear: you cannot have a bad relationship with people and maintain a good relationship with God. Your horizontal human relationships affect your vertical spiritual relationship with God.

Jesus told His followers that attempts at making peace would need to be taken before they could freely and fully worship God. In fact, He even said that their vertical worship of God was to be immediately halted until attempts were made to resolve a personal conflict with someone else. Only then could they return to worship God.

"Therefore, if you are offering your gift at the altar and there remember that your brother or sister has something against you, leave your gift there in front of the altar. First go and be reconciled to them; then come and offer your gift."
MATTHEW 5:23–24

Jesus teaches that there comes a point when action must be taken, whether we are the offender or the offended. If we are the offender, we are to interrupt our worship in order to go and make things right. In the same way, if we are the offended party because someone has significantly hurt us, we are obligated to go to them privately, share with them how they have hurt us, and seek resolution to the conflict.

> *"If your brother or sister sins, go and point out their fault, just between the two of you. If they listen to you, you have won them over."*
> MATTHEW 18:15

Putting these two passages together, it becomes clear that conflict must not be ignored. Whether we are the offender (Matthew 5:23–34) or the offended (Matthew 18:15) we are to take the initiative to make peace. Ideally both parties will meet in the middle as they run to each other to make things right.

6. Conflict must be handled wisely

Conflict is inevitable. The issue is not *will* you have conflicts in your relationships—you will. The issue is *how* will you handle the conflicts when they arise? People with good relationships handle conflict wisely. People with poor relationships don't. Successful relationships are the result of making peace without leaving scars. Good relationships result from learning to fight fair.

Let's think in terms of marriages. All couples fight. Good couples fight clean. Bad couples fight dirty. Research indicates that "being in love" is a very poor indicator of marital happiness and success. Far more important to the successful survival of a marriage is how well couples handle disagreements.

Unwise Ways to Handle Conflict

After more than twenty years of studying marriages, Dr. John Gottman found a reliable way to track a couple's marital breakdown based on how they handled conflict. He observed four escalating stages of dealing with conflict, which he calls "the Four Horsemen of the Apocalypse." They mark disastrous ways of interacting. I have found that the Four Horsemen affect not only marriages but all relationships.

1. Criticism
There is a difference between a legitimate complaint and an unnecessary criticism. A complaint can serve as a positive step toward resolving a conflict. But criticism only makes a conflict worse. A complaint is objective and attacks a problem, while a criticism is subjective and attacks the other person. A complaint focuses on the other person's behavior, while a criticism focuses on their personality.

According to relationship experts Les and Leslie Parrott, "As a general rule, criticism entails blaming, making a personal attack or an accusation, while a complaint is a negative comment about something you wish were otherwise. Complaints usually begin with the word *I* and criticisms with the word *you*."[2]

2. Contempt

Unresolved issues fester and turn toxic. They are like a spreading cancer as mild irritation becomes outright contempt. If one member of the relationship insults and psychologically abuses the other, everything good in the relationship is overwhelmed by the contemptible acid of name calling, hostile humor, and mockery.[3]

3. Defensiveness

Conflicts are resolved when people take responsibility for their part of the problem. But when criticism and contempt enter the scene, defensiveness arises. Walls are erected to protect, rather than bridges built to connect.

4. Stonewalling

Worn down by attacks, one member in the relationship will shut down and stop responding. The very act of not responding conveys arrogant disapproval, distance, and distrust.

Once these four negative responses to conflict become normal, the relationship becomes very fragile at best. The best scenario is never to start down this ugly path but rather learn to handle conflict wisely and make peace.

Wise Ways to Handle Conflict

1. Overlook

Most things probably aren't worth fighting about. Les and Leslie Parrott tell married couples that 90 percent of the issues they bicker about can be overlooked. The Bible lauds the wisdom of learning to overlook small irritations.

> *A person's wisdom yields patience;*
> *it is to one's glory to overlook an offense.*
> PROVERBS 19:11

> *Fools show their annoyance at once,*
> *but the prudent overlook an insult.*
> PROVERBS 12:16

If you're going to get upset about something, make sure it's something worth getting upset about; because if you choose to get upset over an issue, you must act responsibly to resolve it. So pick your battles wisely.

> *Starting a quarrel is like breaching a dam;*
> *so drop the matter before a dispute breaks out.*
> PROVERBS 17:14

Often the solution to conflict is to choose to be the bigger person and to love unconditionally. Sometimes it's a matter of choosing to extend the same unmerited forgiveness to the other person that the Lord has extended to you.

> *Above all, love each other deeply, because*
> *love covers over a multitude of sins.*
> 1 PETER 4:8

Regarding overlooking an offense, Sande says, as a general rule, if you can answer "no" to the following questions, you can overlook an offense. (If you answer "yes" to any of these questions, the offense is too serious to overlook.)

- Does the offense seriously dishonor God?
- Has it permanently damaged a relationship?
- Is it seriously hurting other people?
- Is it seriously hurting the offender?[4]

2. Get the log out of your eye

Jesus warned us against trying to resolve conflict without first examining ourselves and taking responsibility for our part in the problem.

*"Why do you look at the speck of sawdust in your brother's eye and pay
no attention to the plank in your own eye? How can you say to your brother,
'Let me take the speck out of your eye,' when all the time there is a plank in
your own eye? You hypocrite, first take the plank out of your own eye, and
then you will see clearly to remove the speck from your brother's eye."*

MATTHEW 7:3–5

Sande writes, "There are generally two kinds of 'logs' we need to look for when dealing with conflict. First, you need to ask whether you have a critical, negative, or overly sensitive attitude that has led to unnecessary conflict. . . . The second kind of log you must deal with is actual sinful words and actions. Because you are often blind to your own sins, you may need an honest friend or advisor who will help you take an objective look at yourself and face up to your contribution to a conflict."[5]

We must resist blaming others but rather take responsibility for our own contribution to the conflict. We should confess our sins to those we have wronged. We must ask God to help us change any attitudes and habits that lead to conflict. We must take the initiative to repair any harm we have caused.

3. Make peace

Some things just cannot be overlooked. Sometimes the hurt is too real and the offense too damaging. At this point, as we have seen earlier in this chapter, the wise person will courageously take action to resolve the conflict and make peace (Matthew 5:23–34; 18:15).

When you feel a conflict arising, it is wise to ask yourself if it's something really worth fighting over. If it is, define the issue clearly and share your feelings directly. Be careful to make an objective complaint instead of a personal criticism.

Later in Matthew's Gospel, Jesus provides three important aspects of making peace.

> *If your brother wrongs you, go and show him his fault, between you and him privately. If he listens to you, you have won back your brother.*
> MATTHEW 18:15 AMP

a. Take action

"If your brother wrongs you, go": Approach the other person; don't avoid the conflict. It seems easier to do nothing, but Jesus said that letting our resentment fester is unacceptable.

b. Keep it private

"Show him his fault, between you and him privately": Conflict should be dealt with privately, if possible. Some people won't go to the one who has offended them to try to make peace. Instead they go to someone else who is not a part of the conflict and tell how the other person has hurt them. This is wrong on many levels.

First, it only deepens resentment toward the offender. Second, it slanders the offender to the third party and gives that person a negative view of the offender. It also puts them in a difficult position, especially if they are the offender's friend or family member. Third, if the offender finds out they have been talked about behind their back, it will be more difficult to make peace with them. Fourth, God's command to "make peace" is being disobeyed. Fifth, the problem is still not resolved.

Be sensitive. No one wants to be called out in front of someone else. Approach the other person as you would want to be approached.

c. Seek restoration

"Show him his fault": We must not pretend a conflict doesn't exist or talk about others behind their backs. When an offense is too serious to overlook, God commands us to go and talk to the offender privately and lovingly about the situation. As we do so, we must remember the following guidelines, as suggested by Ken Sande:

- Pray for humility and wisdom
- Plan our words carefully (think of how you would want to be confronted)
- Anticipate likely reactions and plan appropriate responses (rehearsals can be very helpful)
- Choose the right time and place (talk in person whenever possible)

- Assume the best about the other person until you have facts to prove otherwise (Proverbs 11:27)
- Listen carefully (Proverbs 18:13)
- Speak only to build others up (Ephesians 4:29)
- Ask for feedback from the other person
- Recognize your limits (Romans 12:18; 2 Timothy 2:24–26). Only God can change people.[6]

What Now?

Instead of accepting a premature compromise or allowing relationships to wither, we must actively pursue genuine peace and reconciliation. This includes forgiving others as God, for Christ's sake, has forgiven us. It also involves seeking just and mutually beneficial solutions to our differences.

Notes

1. Ken Sande, "The Peacemakers Pledge," http://www.peacemaker.net/site/c.aqKFLTOBIpH/b.958149/k.303A/The_Four_Gs.htm (accessed June 1, 2011). The Peacemaker website gives many helpful tips for conflict resolution. For more details, I suggest that you read Ken Sande's *The Peacemaker*, (Grand Rapids, Baker, 2004).

2. Les and Leslie Parrott, *Saving Your Marriage Before It Starts*, 123.

3. Ibid.

4. Ken Sande, "The Four G's" http://www.peacemaker.net/site/c.aqKFLTOBIpH/b.958149/k.303A/The_Four_Gs.htm (accessed June 1, 2011).

5. Ibid.

6. Ibid.

11

Comfort

Therefore comfort one another with these words.
1 THESSALONIANS 4:18 NKJV

Poor guy. In one horrible, terrible, rotten, no good, very bad day, Job, the richest man on earth, lost it all. All his cattle, sheep, oxen, donkeys, camels, and all but a handful of servants. In twenty-first century language his job, career, company, capital, retirement funds, wealth, and staff vanished.

But that wasn't everything. Beyond the sorrow of seeing everything he had spent his life working for stolen or destroyed, Job lost something even more precious—his children. All ten of them were killed.

And if that were not enough, the only comfort Job's bitter wife offered was the advice to "curse God and die." Even worse, the next day Job lost his health as he awakened with a body covered in swollen, oozing, angry red boils.

Devastated, despairing, deflated, and depressed, he desperately needed a little comfort. Grief-stricken, anguished, crushed, and pummeled with pain, he longed for the comfort of a true friend.

Sadly, none came.

Oh, his "friends" came by but not to comfort Job. They showed up to talk at him but failed to listen to him. Even though they were physically present, they were emotionally distant and completely failed to connect with him. They offered him neither sympathy nor empathy. They failed to help, strengthen, or encourage this broken man. Instead, they criticized and condemned him.

Job said he expected them to offer him hope, but like a barren oasis to a thirsty caravan, they offered him only dust (Job 6:14–20). As comforters he called them "a bunch of pompous quacks" (Job 13:4 MSG). Frustrated, Job eventually could not stand it any longer and cried, "You are miserable comforters, all of you!" (Job 16:2).

Needless to say, their failure to comfort Job in his overwhelming grief, sorrow, and suffering nearly destroyed their relationship. Never underestimate the power of comfort to help another and enhance a relationship.

Secret #11
Comfort others when they are suffering.

An Expert in Suffering

Like Job, the apostle Paul also experienced unimaginable suffering in his life. At one point he reminded the Corinthian Christians that he had been in filthy prisons several times, been flogged severely, and been exposed to death repeatedly. Five times he had received from the Jews the awful whipping called "the forty lashes minus one," in which a man was whipped with a leather whip fixed with pieces of bone and lead so as to inflict the maximum amount of damage (2 Corinthians 11:23–24). Three times he had been beaten with Roman rods. He had been shipwrecked three times and had spent a night and a day in the open sea. He had even been stoned by the Jews but had miraculously survived. He had experienced difficult traveling year after year, which included fording rivers, fending off robbers, being endangered by desert sun and stormy seas, and being betrayed by those he thought were his brothers. He had experienced many long and lonely sleepless nights, many missed meals, and had been cold and naked (2 Corinthians 11:25–27).

On top of all of that, Paul felt the heartache of trying to oversee newborn, struggling churches (2 Corinthians 11:28). None of those churches gave him more grief than the church at Corinth.

Bruised and scarred, Paul's pain-racked legacy of suffering makes his words about comfort and suffering all the more powerful. In fact, he opens his second letter to the Corinthians with a powerful reminder that God comforts us, so that we can comfort others.

> *Praise be to the God and Father of our Lord Jesus Christ, the Father of compassion and the God of all **comfort**, who **comforts** us in all our troubles, so that we can **comfort** those in any trouble with the **comfort** we ourselves receive from God.*
> 2 CORINTHIANS 1:3–4 (EMPHASIS ADDED)

God Comforts Us

1. The Father of compassion

This title for God is the Old Testament language of a sufferer crying out for God to treat him with mercy, kindness, love, and tenderness. Paul opens his talk about comfort and suffering by reminding us that God has a huge heart for the hurting. He is tender with the hurting and near to the brokenhearted.

2. The God of all comfort

When we are blinded by the pain of suffering and struggle to maintain perspective, it is important to remember that God is "the God of all comfort." Later in his letter to the Corinthians, Paul refers to God as the one "who comforts the downcast" (2 Corinthians 7:6).

3. Comfort

Paul uses the word *comfort* nine times in five verses (2 Corinthians 1:3–7). The word Paul selects for "comfort" is a compound word, combining *para*—"to come alongside of"—and *kaleo*—"to call out or invite." It means "called alongside to help." It is not something we can offer others from a safe distance.

The Psalms are full of wonderful statements describing the Lord as the Helper of the afflicted. God is seen as "the helper of the fatherless" (Psalm 10:14), "our help and our shield" (Psalm 33:20), "our refuge and strength, an ever-present help in trouble" (Psalm 46:1).

The term *comfort* is further connected to the Latin root *fortis*, which means "brave." Comfort is not a synonym for "ease, softness, or a settled feeling." It is a synonym for "courage, bravery, and strength." Paul doesn't mean that God comes to the aid of the afflicted and offers them a cushy life. He's saying that God comes alongside the afflicted to give strength, courage, boldness, and bravery.

4. All comfort. . .all our troubles

God is the source of every type of righteous comfort imaginable—strength, wisdom, encouragement, hope, help, mercy, and compassion. When we suffer, God is near. He comes alongside us to comfort us. He does this in all our troubles. His help extends to every area of hardship we encounter. God is our source of comfort.

5. Jesus Christ: Comforter

In his first public sermon, Jesus stood in the synagogue, took the scroll of Isaiah, turned to a prophecy of the coming Messiah, and applied it to Himself. In doing so, He proclaimed He would be the Comforter.

> *The Spirit of the Sovereign Lord is on me, because the Lord has anointed me to proclaim good news to the poor. He has sent me to bind up the brokenhearted, to proclaim freedom for the captives and release from darkness for the prisoners, to proclaim the year of the Lord's favor and the day of vengeance of our God, to **comfort** all who mourn.*
>
> Isaiah 61:1–2 (emphasis added)

Three years later, and hours before His arrest and ultimate crucifixion, Jesus wanted to comfort His disciples. In the coming days, they would need strength, courage, and boldness. Jesus promised that they would be given *another Comforter*, one with the same DNA as Jesus—that is, the Holy Spirit.

> *And I will ask the Father, and He will give you **another Comforter (Counselor, Helper, Intercessor, Advocate, Strengthener, and Standby)**, that He may remain with you forever.*
>
> John 14:16 amp (emphasis added)

*The **Comforter**. . .the Holy Spirit, Whom the Father*
will send in My name [in My place, to represent
Me and act on My behalf], He will teach you all things.
JOHN 14:26 AMP (EMPHASIS ADDED)

Notice how many words the Amplified Bible uses to describe the Comforter—*Counselor, Helper, Intercessor, Advocate, Strengthener,* and *Standby.* God, the Holy Spirit, is available to comfort His children. He gives us courage and strength to face the afflictions before us, no matter what they are. And through the Holy Spirit, He is able to play any role of Comforter we need, be it Counselor, Helper, Intercessor, Advocate, Strengthener, or Standby.

If you are suffering—or, should I say, *when* you are suffering—remember that God is a very present help in time of need. He is the God of all comfort.

Note also that the comfort we receive from God is transferable and intended to be shared.

So We Can Comfort Others

Praise be to. . .the God of all comfort, who comforts us
*in all our troubles, **so that we can comfort those in any***
***trouble** with the comfort we ourselves receive from God.*
2 CORINTHIANS 1:3–4 (EMPHASIS ADDED)

God comforts us in our suffering, in part so that we take the comfort we have received and pass it on to others. He often brings us alongside others who are going through hard times so that we can be there for them just as He was there for us. God comforts us so we can better comfort others.

The suffering we encounter will either involve us with others or isolate us from others. We will either build walls or bridges, depending on the attitude we take. The lessons we learn through suffering become planks in the bridge that leads to the hearts of others.

Rick Warren writes,

If you really desire to be used by God, you must understand a powerful truth: The very experiences that you have resented or regretted most in life—the ones you've wanted to hide and forget—are the experiences God wants to use to help others. They are your ministry![1]

Our suffering, and the comfort we experience in it, becomes the key to our ministry.

D. James Kennedy was a popular pastor and media preacher. Regarding the power of suffering to enable us to better comfort others, he told of a young mother who lost her two-year-old son when he climbed over a fence, fell into a boat canal, and drowned. Kennedy went on to tell how the entire church showed up to minister to the young woman. He writes, "The grief-stricken mother later told me that while she appreciated the outpouring of concern, the presence of three people had comforted her the most: three other mothers who had lost children."[2]

A Fellow-Patient in the Same Hospital

> *Think of me as a fellow-patient in the same hospital who,*
> *having been admitted a little earlier, could give some advice.*
> C. S. LEWIS, LETTER TO SHELDON VANAUKEN[3]

American professor Sheldon Vanauken and his precious wife, Davy, converted to Christianity partly because of the influence of C. S. Lewis. Then, when Davy was forty, she contracted a virus that quickly led to her death. Lewis's words to Vanauken comforted him in the midst of his suffering, deepening their friendship and strengthening Vanauken's faith. Five years later, Lewis suffered his own loss when his wife, Joy, died from bone cancer.

We all go through hard times. We all need comfort. We all need to use the comfort we find in God to comfort others as they suffer.

No One Can Better Encourage an Addict Than an Addict

Alcoholics Anonymous has over two million members worldwide. They hold one another accountable to soberness, helping others do the same. Founded in 1935 in Akron, Ohio, by Bill Wilson and Dr. Bob Smith, one of the secrets to its success lies in the recognition that no one can better encourage an addict than an addict.[4]

Seeking an even more Christian approach, John Baker launched Celebrate Recovery in 1991. People attending don't have to qualify themselves as alcoholics, addicts, or gamblers but can attend if they desire to work through any number of "hurts, hang-ups, and habits."[5]

We have run a large Celebrate Recovery ministry at our church for many years. We expanded it to serve not only those suffering from addictions but also those dealing with grief, bankruptcy, job loss, divorce, and abortion. Our groups are each led by persons who have been on the same side of the fence and have found God's solutions to their "hurts, habits, and hang-ups."

A Pocket Full of Gifts to Share

Sheila Walsh cohosted a popular television show, wrote several successful books, and ministered to large audiences. Yet she felt like she was dying inside. Lonely and depressed, she checked herself into a psychiatric hospital. There she confronted her long-held fears and hurts.

With the experience of a veteran sufferer, she writes, "Some of God's most precious gifts come in boxes that make your hands bleed when you open them."[6] She continues, "You do not come out of the desert empty-handed. You come out with a pocketful of gifts that are to share."[7] And she wisely adds, "Not a moment of our lives is wasted in God's economy."[8]

Regarding the ministry of comfort she concludes,

The words God spoke to me in the desert were to become my loaves and fishes. They formed the lunch that I could bring to Christ in the starving masses of His people.[9]

I Was Willing to Touch Hurting and Broken People

Ruth Graham is the daughter of famous parents—evangelist Billy Graham and his wife, Ruth Bell Graham. She has lived a life with unexpected sorrow and pain and confesses,

My own story is not tidy. Nor is it simple. My story is messy and complicated and still being written. I have known betrayal, divorce, depression, and the consequences of bad judgment. I have struggled to parent my children through crisis pregnancy, drug use, and an eating disorder. I have known heartbreak, desperation, fear, shame, and a profound sense of inadequacy. This is not the life I envisioned. Far from it.[10]

Yet Ruth found comfort in God. Because of her history of anguish, she developed a deep desire to take the comfort God had given her and comfort others who were in pain.

I was willing to touch hurting and broken people with the same grace God had shown me when I was hurting and broken.[11]

Ten Ways to Comfort the Afflicted

1. Go to them in person as soon as possible. If that is impossible, at least call.
2. Put yourself in their shoes. Ask God to help you understand what they are feeling right now.
3. Give them a hug.
4. Say little, listen much. Save long lectures and sermons for another time. They probably don't need information as much as they need consolation.
5. Briefly share how God has comforted you and brought you through your own suffering.
6. Read a scripture that has encouraged you in your suffering.
7. Remind them that as long as God is still breathing, there is still hope.
8. Help them reframe the picture of their affliction and refocus their thinking to a God perspective.
9. Pray for them aloud in their presence as you would want someone to pray for you if you were suffering.
10. Follow up on their progress.

What Now?

Make up your mind to be a comforter. Use your wounds to be a wounded healer. Allow your brokenness to build a bridge to the hearts of others who are hurting.

Notes

1. Rick Warren, *The Purpose Driven Life*, (Grand Rapids, MI: Zondervan, 2002), 247.

2. D. James Kennedy, *Turn It into Gold* (Ann Arbor, MI: Vine Books, 1991), 34.

3. Sheldon Vanauken, *A Severe Mercy* (New York: Harper & Row, 1987), 134.

4. Quoted from, "This is A.A." (New York: Alcoholics Anonymous World Services, 1984), 20.

5. Taken from the home page of the Celebrate Recovery website, http://www.celebraterecovery.com/ (accessed Aug. 14, 2011).

6. Sheila Walsh, "A Winter's Tale," in *The Desert Experience* (Nashville: Thomas Nelson, 2001), 172.

7. Ibid., 178.

8. Ibid., 180.

9. Ibid., 180.

10. Ruth Graham with Stacy Mattingly, *In Every Pew Sits a Broken Heart* (Grand Rapids: Zondervan, 2004), 13.

11. Ibid., 168.

12

Invest

Let no debt remain outstanding, except the continuing debt to love one another, for whoever loves others has fulfilled the law.

ROMANS 13:8

We live in a debt-riddled society. As of March 25, 2011, the total public debt outstanding in the United States of America was $14.26 trillion—that's fourteen trillion, two hundred and sixty million dollars! Overall consumer debt is currently $2.5 trillion. Of that total, $900 billion is consumer credit card debt. The rest is auto loans and student loans, as well as loans on boats, trailers, or even vacations. The average American spends twelve cents out of every dollar earned paying off debt on nonappreciating items. The average American family owes $15,000 in credit card debt alone.

The apostle Paul told the Roman church to pay off all their debts except one—*the continuing debt to love one another*. By putting the concept of loving one another into financial terms, Paul encourages us to practice *relational banking*.

Relational Banking

Paul was a brilliant, stubborn, tough, type A, hard-driven, project-oriented person. At the beginning of his ministry, he struggled with relationships—as seen in his breakup from Barnabas over the inclusion of John Mark to their church planting team. Yet as Paul grew older, he grew wiser. By the end of his life, he had become a master of relationships.

As you know, Paul became a mentor to many young Christian leaders, including Luke, Titus, Silas, and Timothy. You may not be aware that he also mentored several others, including Lucius, Jason, and Sosipater (Romans 16:21); Sosthenes (1 Corinthians 1:1); Tychicus (Ephesians 6:21); Epaphroditus (Philippians 2:25); Onesimus (Colossians 4:9); Aristarchus (Colossians 4:10); Jesus, who is called Justus (Colossians 4:11); Epaphras (Colossians 4:12); Crescens (2 Timothy 4:10); Carpus (2 Timothy 4:13); Erastus and Trophimus (2 Timothy 4:20); Eubulus, Pudens, and Linus (2 Timothy 4:21); and Artemas (Titus 3:12). His letter to the Romans is full of personal greetings to many members of the church—his "dear friends"—including Priscilla, Aquila, Epenetus, Mary, Andronicus, Junia, Ampliatus, Urbanus, Stachys, Apelles, Aristobulus, Herodion, Narcissus, Tryphena, Tryphosa, Persis, Rufus, Asyncritus, Phlegon, Hermes, Patrobas, Hermas, Philologus, Julia, Nereus, and Olympas (Romans 16:3–15).

With so many dear friends and associates, Paul had obviously mastered the art of building relationships. But what was his secret? Again, *relational banking*. Notice that Paul describes his love for the Corinthians in terms of spending and being spent for them.

> *And I will very gladly **spend** and **be spent** for your souls;*
> *though the more abundantly I **love** you, the less I am **loved**.*
> 2 CORINTHIANS 12:15 NKJV (EMPHASIS ADDED)

Secret #12
Invest in others.

Love Is an Investment

Jesus, of course, was a relational genius. So effective was He at building relationships that eleven of His close friends faced persecution, prison, and martyrdom for their loyalty to Him. Dozens of others became committed friends and followers. This is not only because they believed the truth of His words but because they felt the depth of His love. Jesus was a master at relational banking.

In His famous Sermon on the Mount, Jesus links love and treasure. In doing so He shows us that, in many ways, love is an investment.

*Do not store up for yourselves **treasures** on earth, where moths and
vermin destroy, and where thieves break in and steal. But store up
for yourselves **treasures** in heaven, where moths and vermin do
not destroy, and where thieves do not break in and steal.
For where your treasure is, there **your heart** will be also.*
MATTHEW 6:19–21 (EMPHASIS ADDED)

Notice that last phrase—*where your treasure is, there your heart
will be also.* In other words, love is an investment. We invest in
what we love and love what we invest in. Since our calling is to
love people, the key to loving people is investing in them.

Love Banking

Willard F. Harley, in his book *His Needs, Her Needs*, introduces the
idea of a "Love Bank":

*I believe each of us has a Love Bank. It contains many different
accounts, one for each person we know. Each person either makes
deposits or withdrawals whenever we interact with him or her.
Pleasurable interactions cause deposits, and painful interactions
cause withdrawals.*[1]

The way love banking works is very simple: When a person's
relational account is full through many or large positive deposits,

he or she feels loved. The relationship is strong and positive. But when the account is depleted through many or sizable withdrawals, the person will feel unloved. The relationship will be weak and negative.

Harley notes that marriages don't fail through incompatibility as much as they fail because of bankrupt love banks. When the account is empty, the feelings of love are absent. The way to help others feel loved is by making deposits. Deposits are made through meeting needs in the other person's life.

Relationships are most mutually fulfilling and run most smoothly when there is a positive balance in the relational account—the larger the balance, the stronger the relationship. We struggle in relationships when there is little or no equity in the relationship account.

Relationship Investments

1. Actions of assistance
Love is not so much a feeling as it is an action or an expression. Love is acted upon and expressed by seeing a need and extending yourself to meet it.

If anyone has material possessions and sees a brother or sister in need but has no pity on them, how can the love of God be in that person? Dear children, let us not love with words or speech but with actions and in truth.

1 JOHN 3:17–18

Suppose a brother or sister is without clothes and daily food.
If one of you says to them, "Go in peace; keep warm and well fed,"
but does nothing about their physical needs, what good is it?
JAMES 2:15–16

Bonds are created when we help each other. I'm not good at home repairs, so I deeply appreciate the guys who give me assistance. I am a klutz with computers, so I appreciate people like my friend Jack, who used to keep my computer running smoothly.

Bonds are also deepened by helping out. When I left home for college, I left my parents with an empty nest. Later they admitted that, at that time, their marital love banks were very low. As a counseling student, I read about the notion of speaking love languages and making relational investments. When I was home for Christmas break, I tried to listen carefully to each of my parents. I noticed that my mom was especially impressed with acts of service.

One night after dinner, when my mom was not paying attention, I said to my dad, "Watch this." I proceeded to clear the table and do the dishes without being asked. Usually my mom did this task by herself. She was so surprised that she commented on it over and over.

My dad picked up on what had happened. The next night he cleared the table and did the dishes without being asked. It was the first time in a long time he had made the investment of assistance.

Mom was pleasantly delighted. She mentioned that she never felt so loved.

Can washing dishes really be an expression of love? Absolutely! Anything you do to ease the burden of responsibilities weighing on another speaks volumes, especially if helping out is their love language. The words he or she most wants to hear may be, "Let me do that for you." Acts of assistance are a positive investment.

But also be aware that laziness, broken commitments, and making more work for other people tells them that their feelings don't matter. It's a withdrawal from the love bank.

2. Affection

As a young pastor, I spent a year training a pilot group of potential group leaders. All of the men in my group were older than I was and already very committed Christians.

One man had grown up in an alcoholic home, and affection was very difficult for him. He tended to be critical of what I was doing as a pastor. He also worked with our teenagers and was critical of our youth pastor as well. So the youth pastor and I decided to try to "love him out of it." We both began to express our affection for him. Our youth pastor took the physical approach by hugging him, and I took the verbal approach by telling him that I loved him.

One night I gave him a ride home from our group meeting. As he got out of the car I said, "Don't forget, I love you, man." He just looked at me and got out of the car.

The next week I said the same thing, "Don't forget, I love you, man."

He paused for a moment with a puzzled look on his face. Then he slowly said, "Well, my wife likes your wife a lot." Then he got out of the car.

The next week I said it again. "Don't forget, I love you, man."

He looked at me and took a deep breath and said, "My wife and I like you and your wife, too."

The next week I gave it another shot. As he got out of the car, I said, "Don't forget, I love you, man."

He dropped his head, and I noticed a tear on his cheek. The power of genuine affection was getting through.

"I, uh," he stammered and gulped hard, "I love you, too, Pastor."

After that he was a different man. He was still highly disciplined and committed. But the hard edge had been replaced with warmth. He went from being a critic to an advocate. In fact, he later moved to another state and drove his new pastor to distraction by telling him all the good things our youth pastor and I were doing.

Learn to give appropriate affection. It is a positive investment and enhances your relationships. Tell them. Show them. An appropriate handshake, a pat on the back, a kind word, or a hug will go a long way in letting people know that you love them.

3. Affirmation and appreciation

Jesus made sure that His followers felt His love. He made the investment of words. On the night He was betrayed, Jesus, the Messiah, the miracle-working Son of God, spoke words to His followers that must have filled their relational accounts.

> *As the Father has loved me, so have I loved you. . . . Greater love has no one than this: to lay down one's life for one's friends. . . . I no longer call you servants, because a servant does not know his master's business. Instead, I have called you friends, for everything that I learned from my Father I have made known to you.*
>
> JOHN 15:9, 13, 15

Notice carefully what Jesus said. "I have loved you." "I no longer call you servants." "I have called you friends." Coming from the Messiah, these words were incredible statements of affirmation.

Actions don't always speak louder than words. For some, words of affirmation and unsolicited compliments make a major investment. Hearing the words, "I love you," "I believe in you," "You are special," are important. Hearing the reasons behind that love is even better. Abraham Lincoln, a master at relationships, stated, "Everybody likes a compliment."

In the 1930s, Dale Carnegie, a young YMCA teacher, taught a popular class on getting along with people. He taught what he called "the big secret in dealing with people." It was, "Be hearty in approbation [formal appreciation] and lavish in your praise."

In 1936 he wrote *How to Win Friends and Influence People*. The book immediately became a bestseller and, as one of the best-selling books in history, still remains popular today, with sales over fifteen million. In it Carnegie writes, "If some people are so hungry for a feeling of importance that they actually go insane to get it, imagine what miracles you and I can achieve by giving people honest appreciation this side of insanity."[2]

Affirming others builds relationships. Go out of your way to express confidence in others. Show public trust in their abilities and character. Affirm their passion, skills, and efforts.

4. Attention

When my boys were little, they said four particular words more than any others. Do you know what they were? They would climb up the slide and yell, "Daddy, look at me!" They would hang upside down from the monkey bars and shout, "Daddy, look at me!" Or they would come out of my room wearing my clothes on their little boy bodies and scream in delight, "Daddy, look at me!" They wanted attention.

"Look at me" is a phrase used repeatedly by small children. They say it less obviously as they get older, but they still cry out for attention. Often they do things to get attention.

I had a good friend in first grade named Chris. He was a very bright, athletic boy, but he got lost in the shuffle of his parents' divorce and began to act out. One day he coerced me to join him in swinging around the boy's bathroom from stall to stall, screaming like monkeys.

Naturally a teacher heard us, and we got sent to the principal's office. Mr. Crabtree looked over his glasses at Chris and asked my friend why he had done such a thing. Chris smiled and simply said, "To get attention."

Of course, most people in your life will not act out so blatantly to get your attention. But that doesn't mean they don't need it. In order to keep a good balance in our relational banks, we need to give other people our attention. It doesn't usually take very long, but it makes a big difference.

Nothing says "I love you" like our full, undivided attention. For this type of person, being there is critical; but *really* being there—with the TV off, fork and knife down, and all chores and tasks on standby—makes people feel truly special and loved. Distractions, postponed dates, or the failure to listen can be especially hurtful.

Learn to be the giver of attention. Look at people when they speak. Read between the lines when they share concerns. Show interest in their job, their family, and their health. Ask about their day. Notice if they seem distracted or down. Pay more attention to them, and they will pay more attention to you.

Relationship Withdrawals

Just as some actions create relational investments, others are guaranteed withdrawals. These include blind spots to one's own wrong behaviors or attitudes and failing to show empathy and understanding by active listening.

We also make relational withdrawals when we practice *relational legalism* by treating others *exactly* as they treat us. For example, if someone is kind to us, then we are kind to them. If they hurt us, we hurt them back. If they are immature, then we are immature as well. Regarding relational legalism, psychologist Henry Cloud writes,

> *The only way for any relationship to overcome our imperfections is for the receiving party to be "bigger than that," and return grace and truth instead of the injury. Simple fairness will kill any relationship.*[3]

What other kinds of relationship withdrawals are there?

1. Emotional detachment

This makes the other party feel as if they are alone, even though someone is there. To feel close, others need us to be present emotionally. We need to share our needs, vulnerabilities, fears, pain, and dreams.

2. Being controlling

Failing to see the other person as a free person who is able to make their own decisions and have their own desires can crush or infuriate them. Seeing others as an extension of ourselves will result in our trying to control what they think, feel, want, do, value, and believe and is destined to drive them away and ultimately deflate love.

3. Narcissism and perfectionism

Real love can only grow where someone's "real self" can be known and accepted by the other person.

4. Dominating the other person

Adults who are in significant relationships are meant to be equals and share the reality of who they are in a spirit of mutuality. Trying to one-up the other person creates more of a parent-child type of connection. This "I know better" attitude withdraws love, as the person who is "under" feels belittled, controlled, dominated, and disrespected. Resentment grows, and the one being dominated will strive to become independent from the dominating one.

What Now?

Remember, love does not "just happen." It takes work. Part of the work is to make positive deposits in your relational accounts. Get into the habit of avoiding the withdrawals and making the deposits into the lives of the ones you love.

Notes

1. Willard F. Harley Jr., *His Needs, Her Needs: Building an Affair-Proof Marriage* (Grand Rapids: Revell, 2001), 25.
2. Dale Carnegie, *How to Win Friends and Influence People* (New York: Simon & Schuster, 2009), 25.
3. Henry Cloud, "Blocks to Love," http://www.cloudtownsend.com/library /articles/7articles1.php.

13

Carry

I was deluged in a tsunami of pain and tormented by a nightmare that would not relent. Every day brought more bad news.

My mom became very weak over Thanksgiving. We buried her six weeks later.

The son we thought would never rebel began to lie to us.

My father-in-law was diagnosed with terminal lung cancer.

I began to have serious problems with a staff member I had hired for our church.

A publisher reneged on a promise to publish a book I had spent a great amount of time writing.

Another one of our sons was projected to finish no lower than third in the state high school wrestling championships. He was using his wrestling success as a platform to share his testimony. But after a freak ailment and a bizarre referee's decision, he failed to place and was heartbroken.

I was so distracted by it all I ran a red light and totaled my car.

Cathy's dad died fifteen minutes before she could get to his deathbed to say good-bye.

My sister-in-law's marriage started to unravel.

My dad was diagnosed with terminal cancer and needed continual care. Day by day we helplessly watched as he wasted away.

I kept asking God to either hold back the onslaught or at least show us what He was doing.

He did neither.

It got so that I could not sleep more than a few hours at night. I would awaken from bad dreams with an overwhelming sense of dread. I was afraid of what could possibly happen next.

Crushed under the weight of more burdens than I could bear, I sat down with a man I considered to be a good friend. He knew most of what we were going through, and I was sure he would give me some much-needed encouragement. I mentioned some of our struggles and said, "I can really use a friend right now."

I will never forget his response.

"No," he said, "I can't be your friend." Then he stood up and walked out of the room.

Stunned, I could not fathom his coldness. I felt as if he had hit me with a sledgehammer.

Later, after I had regrouped, I contacted him again. I asked what on earth I had done to illicit such a heartless response.

He had me. I was battered and broken. He had the choice. He could either help me carry the burden or add more to it.

He chose the latter.

He coolly pulled out a notebook and read me ten areas of my life and ministry he thought were out of line. Like Job's "friends," instead of lightening the load, he piled more on.

Obviously this did not help me or enhance our relationship. (To his credit, he has since apologized and made efforts to make amends.)

Over the past few years, every time I wanted to get angry at Him, God has reminded me of times when I acted like an unloving jerk, insensitive to someone else's burdens, and failed to help them carry their load. That painful episode made me much more sensitive to people in pain and more aware of how important it is to at least try to help carry the load for someone who is broken by massive burdens.

Carry Each Other's Burdens

Two thousand years ago, the apostle Paul wrote to the church of Galatia. They were caught up in self-righteous legalism, and their fellowship was suffering as a result. Paul gave them sage advice.

*Let us not become conceited, provoking and envying each other. Brothers and sisters, if someone is caught in a sin, you who live by the Spirit should restore that person gently. But watch yourselves, or you also may be tempted. **Carry each other's burdens**, and in this way you will fulfill the law of*

Christ. If anyone thinks they are something when they are not, they deceive themselves. Each one should test their own actions. Then they can take pride in themselves alone, without comparing themselves to someone else, for each one should carry their own load.
GALATIANS 5:26–6:5 (EMPHASIS ADDED)

Secret #13
Carry others' burdens.

Paul's letter to the Galatians gives us helpful insights on helping others with their burdens. Let's look at what he says and then dig deeper so we can apply it to our relationships.

Lift Heavy Loads

There seems to be a contradiction between Galatians 6:2 ("carry each other's burdens") and Galatians 6:5 ("each should carry their own load"), but there is not. In verse 2 the word *burdens* refers to "a heavy load, a crushing trial, a weight too great to bear alone." In verse 5 the word *load* speaks of "a load small enough to be carried on your back," and refers to a soldier's backpack.

There are some responsibilities I must bear on my own. I

am responsible to be the husband and father in my home. I am responsible to carry out the tasks God has called me to fulfill. As verse 5 says, I need to shoulder my own responsibilities.

There are also some concerns that are common to life on planet earth. We all face a regular dose of small but annoying troubles, trials, and tribulations. We need to carry on in spite of them.

But verse 2 speaks of those burdens that are simply too great to be carried alone. Trying to shoulder them crushes the person underneath the weight. These burdens can refer to the pulverizingly heavy burdens that often come in this life—sickness, unemployment, loss of a loved one, loneliness, and rejection. As a pastor, I regularly saw people crushed by such heavy loads.

Sometimes there was no one to blame. A family breadwinner loses hope after losing his job and being unable to find another. A usually upbeat young lady staggers from the doctor's office stunned with the news that she has breast cancer. A single mom is overwhelmed by the added load of caring for her sick and aging parents. A fire destroys the family home.

Sometimes our burdens are caused by the sins of others. Parents grieve as their beloved daughter is killed by a drunk driver. A couple is racked with shame and guilt when their teenage son is arrested for drug use. Another couple pulls away from everyone else, embarrassed that their fifteen-year-old daughter is pregnant. A wife is crushed to find pornography on her husband's computer. A husband is broken when his wife asks for a divorce. A young husband comes home from work early to find his wife in the arms of another man. A pastor is exhausted by battling a litany of costly legal trials and IRS audits stemming from false accusations by a disgruntled member. A family is in financial turmoil as the father is fired for embezzling a large sum of money and must pay it back or go to jail.

In many cases, who is to blame is not the issue. It is the weight of the load that matters. All of these are crushing loads that no one can carry alone. Our responsibility is to notice, stop, bend down, and reach out to help the overwhelmed and oppressed lift their load and carry it. We must develop the extraordinary skill for detecting the burdens of others and making them lighter.

Help Out the Weak

Carrying the burdens of others is often rather simple.

Sometimes all that is needed is taking just a minute to listen, offer words of encouragement, put your hand on their shoulder, and pray for them. You can also ask how you might help, and check in regularly so they do not feel so alone in their pain.

On other occasions, burden-bearing may be more complicated and costly. It may take writing a large check to cover someone's unexpected bill or taking time every week to drive someone to a doctor's appointment. It may require making some phone calls on behalf of an elderly man. It could cost an evening as you watch a hurting young couple's small children and give them money for a date night. Or it may require doing the weekly yard work of a recent widow or the housework of a widower.

Several years ago my good friend Joan and her family experienced a crushing nightmare. As Joan was pulling out of a grocery store parking lot, her vehicle was crushed by an eighteen-wheeler. Flown to a hospital, Joan was not expected to live. She was a mess of broken bones, including a fractured skull. She had experienced a traumatic brain injury.

I will never forget going to the hospital that night. When I was finally allowed to see her, I couldn't remember ever seeing a human look less human. Blood, swelling, bandages, tubes, and machines combined to create a macabre scene. As I recall that night and try to write this chapter, I cannot help choking back tears. As a pastor, I have seen numerous people lying in intensive care units, but Joan was probably in the worst shape of all. I did not see how she would live through it, and if she did, I was sure her disabilities would ensure that she would never have a very high quality of life.

Over the next few years, we saw God do many amazing things. Many members of our church helped Joan and her family carry the crushing load of rebuilding their lives. In a letter she wrote to me, Joan said,

My church acted as the hands and feet of Christ. My family got meals each night from January until my kids got out of

school in June. My house was cleaned each week by teams of women from the church until I could manage it myself. I also had two women a day who sat with me once I came home. I could not be left alone because of the swallowing problem. This was such a huge amount of volunteerism, but I was never, ever made to feel like anybody minded the extra work.[1]

Since then Joan has experienced an almost complete recovery. Her marriage has been enriched and her love for the body of Christ deepened.

Restore the Fallen

*Brothers and sisters, if someone is caught in a sin, you who live by the Spirit should **restore that person gently**. But watch yourselves, or you also may be tempted. Carry each other's burdens, and in this way you will fulfill the law of Christ.*

GALATIANS 6:1–2 (EMPHASIS ADDED)

The context of burden bearing is restoring people who have been overwhelmed by their sin. Their failure to resist temptation has created overwhelming burdens. Our obligation is to lighten their load and gently restore them.

We must act. We must help people get out of their sin and put their lives back together. Certainly we would not merely walk by a person who has stumbled and fallen into a dangerous place. We would make every effort to go to them, reach down, pick them up, and help carry them out. This is exactly what Paul says we must do for one another spiritually.

When someone falls into sin, we must not rejoice over their downfall or reveal their sin to others. No. We are called to *restore* them. The word *restore* speaks of mending a torn net, equipping an army, outfitting a ship for a voyage, setting a broken bone, or polishing a person's character.

The manner of restoration is *gentleness*. The motive is *love*. The purpose is to help the fallen get up and get going so they can become spiritually useful again. The means is humble confrontation and ongoing accountability. Accountability is a tool and gift we use to help others resume their lives stronger than before.

I have a friend—I'll call him Keith—who wanted to be a leader in our church. Part of the leadership development process involved mentoring and accountability from a more advanced leader. Keith's mentor was to be Tom (also not his real name). As this process began, it became evident to Tom that Keith had some potentially problematic moral and marriage issues. Eventually he asked Keith point-blank if he was being unfaithful to his wife.

Keith denied it, but he was unconvincing.

Tom asked me to sit in on their next meeting. Together we confronted Keith with patterns of behavior that pointed to adultery. Reluctantly he admitted it but seemed unrepentant. When we pointed out the seriousness of adultery, Keith broke down before God and repented of his sin. Over the next few weeks, we led him through a process of completely removing himself from the immoral relationship. We coached him on how to rebuild his marriage and renew his walk with God.

Tom provided Keith with loving, consistent accountability to continue on the right path until thinking and doing right became Keith's lifestyle. Eventually Keith was fully restored and became the spiritually effective leader and godly husband and father he wanted to be.

Examine Yourself

*Let us not become conceited, provoking and envying each other. Brothers and sisters, if someone is caught in a sin, you who live by the Spirit should restore that person gently. But **watch yourselves**, or you also may be tempted. Carry each other's burdens, and in this way you will fulfill the law of Christ. If anyone thinks they are something when they are not, they deceive themselves. **Each one should test their own actions**.*
GALATIANS 5:26–6:4 (EMPHASIS ADDED)

The way we view ourselves determines the way we will treat others. In this passage about helping the weak and restoring the fallen, Paul says to "watch ourselves" and "test our own actions." We need to treat the weak, the fallen, and the burdened as we would like someone to treat us *if we were in the same situation*. We should treat them humbly and gently, with dignity and grace. Otherwise we will needlessly add to the burdens of the weak and the fallen.

Paul identifies four actions that fail to remove the burden from the weak or to restore the fallen. These must be avoided as we carry each other's burdens.

1. No selfish competition

Friends who effectively carry the burdens of others are selfless in their attitude and approach. They don't use the other person's suffering for their own benefit. They are not "conceited, provoking and envying each other" (Galatians 5:26).

2. No criticizing from a distance

Effective burden bearers refuse to act superior to the hurting person. They never act too good or too important to stoop down and get their hands dirty. Instead they recognize their own areas of spiritual struggle, watching themselves so they are not tempted (Galatians 6:1) and refusing to see themselves as something they are not (Galatians 6:3).

3. No condemning

Instead of heaping self-righteous condemnation on the suffering person, effective burden bearers judge themselves (Galatians 6:4). They recognize that we all struggle in life. They are aware of the fact that if they aren't suffering right now it is more a testimony of God's goodness and grace than anything they have done or deserve.

4. No controlling

Holding someone accountable does not mean we view ourselves as being in control of their lives. The effective burden bearer is gentle in attitude and approach. Gentleness does *not* mean being passive, retiring, or uninvolved. It also doesn't mean using the other person's plight as an excuse to control them. The gentle person is not harsh, severe, or abusive. He or she doesn't patronize or speak down to others. Instead the gentle person is equitable, moderate, fair, forbearing, and kind.

No selfish competition, criticizing, condemning, or controlling. No one should be kicked when they are down. Instead they should be gently, yet firmly, lifted up and helped to get going again. Treating the weak and fallen with humility, grace, and gentleness enables us to really help them.

Remember: Love Is the Key

> *Brothers and sisters. . .carry each other's burdens,*
> *and **in this way you will fulfill the law of Christ.***
> GALATIANS 6:1–2 (EMPHASIS ADDED)

By carrying the burdens of others we "fulfill the law of Christ." Paul explains what this means when he writes, "For the entire law is fulfilled in keeping this one command: 'Love your neighbor as yourself'" (Galatians 5:14). The key is love.

> *Serve one another humbly **in love**. For **the entire law** is fulfilled in*
> *keeping this one command: "**Love your neighbor as yourself.**"*
> *If you bite and devour each other, watch out or you*
> *will be destroyed by each other.*
> GALATIANS 5:13–15 (EMPHASIS ADDED)

The Galatians were legalistic people, more interested in rules and rituals than relationships. They tended to focus on the external instead of the internal. Paul warned them not to "bite and devour each other" in crippling criticism and condemnation (Galatians 5:15) but instead to "serve one another humbly in love" (Galatians 5:13). The key to getting along with others is always love. Helping the weak and restoring the fallen is ineffective without it.

What Now?

Burden bearing is the command of God for the loving Christian. Drop your pride and judgmentalism. Stoop down and help others lift their loads. Take every opportunity to help the weak and restore the fallen.

Notes

1. Joan Angus, personal correspondence with the author. Used with permission.

14

Endure

Be patient, bearing with one another in love.
EPHESIANS 4:2

I t was often a nightmare that would not end.

Bouncy, bright, cute, happy, sensitive, funny—he was the most wonderful little boy you could imagine. Yet it all began to unravel.

When his beloved grandmother died, he got mad at God.

Then, when he was leading a Bible study at his middle school, some of the kids twisted something he said. The next thing he knew, he was shunned as the kids turned on him, accusing him of being a Jew hater. He grew even angrier at God.

His older brother was a star athlete and his younger brother was the genius scholar, but who was he? Why hadn't God given him any special abilities like his brothers?

Insomnia ruined his nights and made him exhausted during the day. When he finally found sleep, he was stunned out of it as dark dreams woke him up sweating and scared. His thoughts grew more and more irrational. What was wrong with him?

When he was a high school freshman, a senior offered him alcohol, and he felt unable to refuse. He found the one thing he was good at—drinking. Even though he weighed just over a hundred pounds, he could outdrink everyone else. So he dove in headfirst. The next few years became a blurry daily battle with alcohol and drug addiction.

His parents were often at their wit's end. Their once sweet, lovable Christian son was defiant and vulgar. He disagreed with everything they said and stood for. He lied to them over and over again. They never knew what to expect as his bipolar personality kept him bouncing perpetually between mania and depression. The conflict between the life he was living and the life he had been taught kept him in a state of debilitating anxiety. His parents followed him into the psych ward, the emergency room, the courtroom, and the jail. He embarrassed his family in front of their friends and hurt their reputation in the community. Yet what really bothered his parents was the ongoing fear of one day finding him dead from an overdose or suicide.

But God gave them the grace to endure. They were patient, bearing with their wayward son in love. They wept and prayed and cried out to God. They fought to stay in his life and kept on loving, kept on forgiving, kept on talking, and kept on listening. They continued to love even when he was so unlovable.

Slowly his hard heart began to turn. Yet his secret life of sin continued.

One night it came to a head. He called home drunk and disoriented. After hours of searching for him, his parents miraculously found him lying unconscious in the middle of a parking garage, sixty miles from home.

He awoke the next morning embarrassed and ashamed. This could not continue. Within a few days the prodigal ran to God, broken and repentant.

The loving Father took him up in his arms and forgave him.

The bouncy, bright, cute, happy, sensitive, funny boy was back—but much deeper and much wiser. He has told his story in many churches with powerful results and is studying to be a pastor today. Never underestimate the value and power of patient, long-suffering forbearance and enduring love.

Secret #14
Endure.

People are imperfect. Relationships are hard, messy, and challenging. Getting along with others stretches us, sometimes to the very end of ourselves.

In our self-centered, consumer-driven culture, we tend to view relationships as conveniences that exist to meet our needs and improve our lot in life. When the going gets tough, we bail. As a result, too many people go through life having only a few very shallow relationships. They experience only superficial acquaintances because they do not understood the essential value of endurance in relationships.

Good relationships do not just happen. They take intentional effort over a period of time. They take commitment and hard work. They take endurance.

Endurance = Long-suffering + Forbearance + Love

Paul certainly was a man who understood suffering and endurance. Because of his passionate commitment to Jesus, he had been locked in filthy prisons, flogged, beaten, and even stoned. He suffered through shipwreck. He had been hungry, cold, and frequently placed in danger (2 Corinthians 11:23–27).

Wisely, he applied the notion of endurance to the area of relationships. He encouraged the Christians of Ephesus to "be patient, bearing with one another in love" (Ephesians 4:2). He skillfully selected several words to help us better comprehend the value of endurance in relationships.

1. Long-suffering

Be patient, bearing with one another in love.
EPHESIANS 4:2 (EMPHASIS ADDED)

The first imperative Paul gives is "Be patient with one another." The word *patient* is somewhat timid sounding in our culture, but in the first century it was a strong word. It spoke of being "constant, steadfast, persevering, and long-suffering." One of the keys to healthy, strong relationships is the quality of "long-suffering." The original meaning of the word involved a person who was "long of soul" or "long of breath." It speaks of *fortitude*. As used by Paul, it indicates *courageously hanging in there with people, even when it hurts.*

God is the author and ultimate example of long-suffering. Numbers 14:18 states, "The LORD is slow to anger, abounding in love and forgiving sin and rebellion." Psalm 86:15 affirms, "But you, Lord, are a compassionate and gracious God, slow to anger [long-suffering], abounding in love and faithfulness."

Of course, God is also the source of our ability to experience and express long-suffering. Galatians 5:22 tells us that "the fruit of the Spirit is. . .forbearance" (another word for *long-suffering*). God promises that He will strengthen us "with all might, according to His glorious power, for all patience and *longsuffering* with joy" (Colossians 1:11 NKJV).

When friends get on our nerves, children let us down, spouses become difficult, and work associates go behind our backs, God's long-suffering heart can control our attitudes and actions if we will yield to His power. When loved ones break our hearts, God can give us the grace to suffer through as long as it takes.

2. Forbearance

> **Bearing with** one another in love.
> EPHESIANS 4:2 (EMPHASIS ADDED)

The second imperative Paul gives us is "bearing with one another in love." The word *bear* is also a very strong word. It comes from a root meaning "to hold." It means "to stand erect and firm, hold up, forbear, and sustain." As used here, it speaks of making allowances for others and supporting them. It suggests holding up as they wear us down and holding them up when they fall down. Forbearance is *bravely putting up with others even when they irritate, annoy, or hurt us, to help them stand up again.*

3. Love

> *Be patient, bearing with one another **in love**.*
> Ephesians 4:2 (emphasis added)

Patience and forbearance are to be motivated by and done in a spirit of *love*—that is, "the unconditional, active effort to do what is best for others." You won't suffer long with people if you don't love them.

Keys to Practicing Endurance in Relationships

1. Hang in there

I have led group home Bible studies almost every week of my life since I was in high school. I have led them in various parts of the country with a diversity of people groups. Over time I have been a part of groups that were very close and committed and groups that were little more than a collection of people who met together for an hour once a week.

In order for a group to become strong and deeply connected, the members must *endure together* through an inevitable and painful process. Friendships, families, and marriages follow a similar path. The key to reaching true community is hanging in there all the way through the process.

Psychologist and professor Dr. Bruce Tuckman spent his

professional life studying group dynamics. He discovered that groups who reach a place of authentic intimacy pass through four primary stages.[1] These stages are true of friendships, families, and marriages as well.

a. Forming

This is the comfortable stage. Controversy is avoided and serious issues are skirted. Conversation revolves around safe facts but not feelings.

b. Storming

This is where the relationship begins to get uncomfortable. Differences of opinion and conflicting values begin to surface. Too often people bail on relationships at this point because it is not easy, especially for those adverse to conflict. But when both parties hang in there through the storming period, and if acceptance and honor are practiced, intimacy is enhanced.

c. Norming

At this point "I" begins to be traded in for "we" and "us." People learn how to get along and make the relationship work.

d. Performing

At this stage the individuals become *inter*dependent. Properly communicated disagreement is allowed and even appreciated within the context of love.

In the context of Christian relationships, I see a fifth stage—*transforming*. As we endure with others through the process, we move from separate entities to a close-knit unit. We move into the joy of deeper relationships. We become more sensitive, humble, and loving people.

Whether we are talking about becoming a fully functional team, a great small group, a strong house church, a close friend, a loving family, or a good married couple, the key is the same. We must hang in there with each other and go through the process. It will get messy and uncomfortable for a period, but the rewards are worth the hassle.

Too many church groups, work teams, married couples, parents and teens, and potential friends bail out too quickly and easily. The rewards of intimacy and community only come as a result of enduring through the process.

2. Take time

We live in an instant age, a consumer culture. We are constantly bombarded with messages telling us that things should be easier, more convenient, and faster. They should take minimal effort and deliver maximum pleasure in return. Yet relationships are not *products*. They are crafted, not purchased. Though speed and easy accessibility are good characteristics for an Internet provider, trying to "do" relationships quickly can be devastating.

Many people would say they don't have time for relationships. But Americans now spend a hundred hours a year commuting to work and have a national average drive time of more than twenty-four minutes. Those who live in large metro areas and commute an hour or more will spend more than 250 hours a year commuting.

Add the fact that the average American watches four hours of television a day. This means the typical husband and wife spend three or four times as much time watching television as they spend talking to each another.

Although few of us would admit that watching television is more important than investing in relationships, our calendars and time logs show otherwise. Simple observation says that television is more important to us than people.

In recent years, more and more people have begun to connect with others through Facebook or other forms of social media. These tools are great for maintaining width of relationships with many people. But what about depth? Texting and Facebooking are no substitute for talking and listening to the people who are supposed to be close to us.

Good marriages, deep friendships, and close families don't just happen. According to psychologist Alan Loy McGinnis, great relationships are the result of a deceptively simple commitment: *Assign top priority to your relationships.*[2]

It is impossible to fit deep relationships into the cracks of an overly busy schedule. We cannot experience community in a hurry. As John Ortberg notes, "Wise people do not try to microwave friendship, parenting, or marriage."[3]

The early church did not have long commutes to eat up their time or television to distract them, so they invested themselves in relationships. Instead of short texts, they enjoyed long conversations. They spent unhurried time listening to, talking to, and praying for one another, and serving and sharing together. As a result, the first Christians experienced an incredibly enriching and attractive community. God smiled on it, and others wanted what they had. As you read Luke's account of their lives, note the centrality of fellowship and the amount of time they devoted to relationships.

*They **committed themselves to** the teaching of the apostles, **the life together, the common meal**, and the prayers. Everyone around was in awe—all those wonders and signs done through the apostles! And **all the believers lived in a wonderful harmony**, holding everything in common. They sold whatever they owned and pooled their resources so that each person's need was met. **They followed a daily discipline** of worship in the Temple followed by **meals at home**, every meal a celebration, exuberant and joyful, as they praised God. People in general liked what they saw. Every day their number grew as God added those who were saved.*

ACTS 2:42–47 MSG (EMPHASIS ADDED)

Their deep fellowship was the result of a daily commitment to God and to each other. It came from a regular, unhurried investment of *time*. It grew out of daily doses of sharing corporate worship and meals together. And the ones on the outside saw what they had and wanted it. What a novel approach to church growth!

3. Don't give up or give in

We're all very busy. When relationships become difficult or costly, it is easy to give up on them. Many of us throw in the towel too quickly.

I want to encourage you to be different. Refuse to give up hope. My friend Daniel Henderson writes, "As long as God's character of long-suffering does not change (and it never will), and as long as His Spirit lives in our hearts (and we are 'sealed' in this assurance), we can believe that God is able to impart all we need for the positive progress of a relationship. He is able to change hearts and lives. We should always let Him start with our own—then trust Him to do the same for others."[4]

Even when we don't give up, we often give in to negative emotions. Our thoughts become irrational and our words unloving. We react in ways we later regret. When the other person is being a pain or causing you pain, don't trust your emotions. It has been noted that "emotions have no brains." Don't allow your emotions to rush beyond the controlling power of the Holy Spirit.

What Now?

Relationships are a gift from God that must be treasured and embraced even when they become difficult and painful. Enduring through tough relationships requires long-suffering, forbearance, and love.

A convenient life is seldom a life of deep character. It is in the fire that we are refined and made strong. Sometimes this refinement involves a demanding marriage, a rebellious child, an unreasonable boss, or a less-than-perfect fellow Christian. These relationships may not be easy—but they are worth it because God uses them to make us more like Jesus.

A convenient relationship is seldom a relationship of deep joy. It is in the fire that rough-edged relationships are refined and made strong. These relationships may not be easy—but they are worth it because God works to make them stronger, deeper, and more rewarding!

Notes

1. Bruce W. Tuckman, "Developmental Sequence in Small Groups," *Psychological Bulletin*, 63, (1965) 384–399.

2. Alan Loy McGinnis, *The Friendship Factor* (Minneapolis: Augsburg, 1979), 22.

3. Ortberg, *Everybody's Normal*, 46.

4. Daniel Henderson, "The Value of Suffering in Relationships," StrategicRenewal.com, April 17, 2011; http://www.strategicrenewal.com/strategic-renewal-e--devotional/the-value-of-suffering-in-relationships.

Conclusion

Putting It All Together

I am licensed as a church consultant. When doing a consultation, I spend weeks gathering all the information I can about the church, do a detailed church health assessment, try to determine the strengths and weaknesses, and offer a plan for getting healthy. Doing it well requires paying the price to get enough information to make an accurate assessment. It takes brainstorming out a plan that will work. Most of all, it takes the guts to tell the church the truth and the faith to give them hope

My sincere desire is that this book has been a positive challenge to take your relational health to the next level. Now I want to help you put together what you have learned so you can become the relationally effective person you desire to be.

But first, I must make a confession. As I studied these fourteen secrets to better relationships, I was more challenged than I expected to be. They motivated me to really amp up *my* relational skills. Now the questions are, "What are the main areas *I* need to focus on now?" "What am *I* going to do about it?" "What specific steps of application will *I* follow through on?" and, "How will *I* find the time to do it?"

Inspiration and information without application leads to

frustration. But information with application produces transformation. This may be the most important part of this book, because it helps you apply what you have learned. Grab a pen and prayerfully take the time to fill out the inventories and assessments in this chapter. As you do, don't be overwhelmed. Rather, be motivated and directed to make a few applications that will help you best grow in your relationships.

Relational Inventory

Respond *yes* or *no* to each statement as honestly as possible:

1. I firmly believe I need others.

2. I know I have experienced the astounding acceptance available in Christ, because I have believed in the fact that Jesus was rejected and died for my sin so I could be accepted by God.

3. Because Jesus has accepted me, I have a heart of acceptance toward other people, even the poor, crooked, and sinful.

4. I am increasingly becoming a more loving person.

5. I choose to love, even when it is costly.

6. I value others highly and give preference to them above myself.

7. I am willing to make others look good, even at my own expense.

8. I humbly live like a person who has nothing to prove, nothing to lose, and nothing to hide.

9. I regularly set aside my rights and privileges to actively serve others.

10. I have learned to view conflict as an assignment with potential for good and not an accident that can only be bad.

11. When conflict arises, I refuse to criticize, defend myself, or shut down.

12. When conflict arises, I take wise steps to make peace.

13. I have several close same-gender relationships.

14. I have at least one or two people with whom I feel safe confessing my sins and receiving prayer.

15. I know I have received the costly, unconditional forgiveness of God for my sins.

16. I consistently extend the same type of costly, unconditional forgiveness to others who hurt me.

17. I am not harboring hard feelings toward anyone else.

18. I consistently pray for my loved ones.

19. The majority of my prayers for others are focused on their spiritual progress.

20. I understand the importance of encouragement and try to live as an encourager.

21. I have recently encouraged someone else by expressing belief in them; setting them up for success, not failure; telling them they are doing a good job; pointing out something they did right; speaking highly of them in front of others.

22. I have learned to find my comfort in God and to pass it along to others.

23. I have recently come alongside of someone who is hurting to give strength, courage, and boldness.

24. My relational accounts are all strong and growing.

25. I look for ways to positively invest in relationships.

26. I consistently shoulder my own responsibilities.

27. Recently I have gone out of my way to help someone who is being overwhelmed with big burdens.

28. I have helped walk someone in sin through the process of restoration.

29. I stick it out when relationships get difficult.

30. I am enduring through a tough relationship with God-given patience, forbearance, and love.

Relationship Assessment

Read back over your responses to the Relational Inventory. Circle the numbers of all the ones where your answer was negative. For example, as I read this manuscript and worked through the inventory, I realized I needed to be more active in honoring others, especially in how I use my words and spend my time. I need to value others more highly and give preference to them above myself.

As you prayerfully consider each negative response, pick a few areas where you are confident the Lord wants you to make changes. Write those areas needing change below:

1.

2.

3.

4.

5.

Relationship Application

Looking back over the areas that you need to change, find the chapter that addresses that area of relationship. For example, as I took the inventory, I realized I am harboring hard feelings toward someone I work with. He is arrogant, annoying, and self-centered, but I need to love him like Jesus loves me, forgive him as Jesus has forgiven me, and pray for him as Jesus prays for me.

Now brainstorm specific steps you can take to improve these areas of relational weakness. Write a brief plan for how you will implement these steps.

1.

2.

3.

4.

5.

A joy-filled life and solid relationships go hand in hand. Real relationships are worth the time and effort. Expend the necessary energy to apply these biblical secrets for better relationships. You will be very glad you did.

Notes

Notes

Notes

....

....

....

....

....

....

....

....

....

....

....

Notes

Notes

....

....

....

....

....

....

....

....

....

....

....